Opportunities to relax (Benton Grange School in the 1960s)

Yesterday's Answers

A Whiting & Birch Ltd / SCA (Education) Co-Publication

Yesterday's Answers:

Development and decline of schools for young offenders

Jim Hyland

Whiting and Birch Ltd

MCMXCIIII

\

Published by Whiting & Birch Ltd, PO Box 872, Forest Hill, London SE23 3HL, England.
USA: Paul & Co, Publishers' Consortium Inc, PO Box 442, Concord, MA 01742.

British Library Cataloguing in Publication Data.
A CIP catalogue record is available from the British Library

ISBN 1 871177 43 X (cased)
ISBN 1 871177 69 3 (limp)

Printed in England by Bourne Press, Poole

Dedication

TO YOUNG PEOPLE EVERYWHERE,

ESPECIALLY CLAIRE, HELEN & THOMAS

Contents

Acknowledgements

This book would not have been possible without the aid and co-operation of many people. In particular I would wish to acknowledge the following:

The senior staff of local authorities and voluntary agencies who responded to my requests for information;

John Gittins, Barbara Kahan and Joan Cooper, all of whom gave me some of their valuable time so that I could discuss with them the events in which they played key roles;

Some former Heads of CHEs with whom I was able to discuss closures or who sent written responses on the subject;

Maurice Logan Salton for sharing with me the outcome of his correspondence on closures;

Sydney Jones for allowing me to use his records of the closure of Polebrook CHE;

Haydn Davies Jones for sharing with me his wealth of knowledge of the history and development of the schools for young offenders and for his constructive comments on my original MEd study of the subject;

The Controller of Her Majesty's Stationery Office who kindly agreed to the reproduction of short extracts from HMSO publications;

Barnados, The Royal Philanthropic Society, The Order of the Good Shepherd and to Catholic Care North East for agreeing to the publication of the photographs from their former establishments.

Nancy Loffler for her painstaking checking of the text which enabled me to correct and clarify. Any remaining errors or omissions however are entirely my own responsibility.

Foreword

BARBARA KAHAN

This book is a historical study written by one of the history makers. Jim Hyland, the author, was deeply involved in approved schools while they were changing to community homes with education. He was part of their struggle for survival in a rapidly changing environment, yet detached enough to examine and analyse the process and record it with care and understanding. It is the first time that the full 150 years of this residential service for young offenders and troubled children has been traced in detail. In the mid 19th century they provided for children who would otherwise have been transported, hanged or sent to 'the hulks'. After many changes in this century, particularly in the 1980s, there is confusion about the role of the handful of CHEs which remain.

The book is being published at a time when the two main political parties in the UK are vying for ascendancy as the party of law and order, defender of victims against 'villains' and the promoter of 'basic values'. As crime figures appear to rise relentlessly, cries of 'bring back the birch, flog them and restore hanging' whip up an emotional climate on chat shows and in party conferences. At the same time unprecedented marital breakdown rates, peak unemployment, lack of adequate housing, constant change in education, health and social services exacerbate children's and families' problems. Cuts in resources and low morale in public services diminish the energy and resourcefulness needed to prevent or counter juvenile offending.

Yesterday's Answers traces the development from the 1850s of a range of residential schools offering care, control and education to delinquent and other needy children. It describes their heyday in the first half of this century and their decline since the mid 1970s following the Children and Young Persons Act 1969 and the establishment of social services departments.

It is a fascinating account of a hybrid system, part voluntary organisations, part local authorities, initially controlled through central government and a mixture of education and child care but not truly part of either service. Its jealously guarded separatism gave it power in some respects, but meant when the twin forces of negative professional opinion and economic pressure were felt that it had few allies. At a time when it most needed to be united in its primary objectives, internal struggles over lesser issues like pay, conditions of work and a continuing degree of autonomy wasted time and effort on short term gains and allowed piecemeal demolition to proceed almost imperceptibly.

The study is one which can be read for its historical interest in the ebb and flow of voluntary services in their relationship to the state; as a study of the lack of realistic national programmes to prevent juvenile delinquency or to help young offenders and their families; or as a study of the quirks, accidental factors and limited perspectives which affect humanitarian enterprises of many kinds. Students of local and central government politics would find it an interesting case study in which at times the outcomes for the young people and the staff working with them seem almost irrelevant.

As someone who has shared the outcomes with the children and the staff and been closely involved with some of the history, the author maintains a high degree of objectivity which must have been, at times, a painful achievement.

Barbara Kahan

Introduction

One of the perennial problems of modern times is that of juvenile delinquency, both in terms of its causes and its management. This publication is primarily an account of the way in which society has, in the last 150 years or so, responded to the dilemma of dealing with young offenders, with particular reference to institutional services. Although it is not within the scope of this work to consider the causes of criminal behaviour, it would be remiss not to acknowledge that this is a fundamental issue. Poverty, bad housing, unemployment, increased availability of material goods, reduced social supervision (e.g. railway stations without staff), the weakening of family structures and a loss of belief in moral and religious systems must all be contributory factors to the growth of crime.

We live in times when it is often difficult to keep abreast of the pace of events. Change and innovation have almost become the norm, if not an obsession. This is indicative of the speed of progress in many areas but it may also sometimes be a case of change for its own sake. This cult of the new can result in a tendency to cast aside existing wisdom, structures and practices with the minimum of reflection.

There have been major developments in the philosophy and systems for dealing with juvenile delinquents in the last 15 years. The greatly increased emphasis on managing young offenders in their own communities and the diversion of juveniles from court are generally welcome trends. What must be a cause for concern, however, is that crime continues to become more prevalent and the fact that many of the offenders are children and young people. There is no room, then, for complacency in respect of present policies and practice in dealing with juvenile delinquency. Despite sustained efforts - the latest being the introduction of the Criminal Justice Act 1991 - to arrive at an effective and just system, the growth of crime continues to be a serious problem in our modern society.

There was a similar anxiety about the growth and prevalence of crime at the beginning of the nineteenth century. Social structures and the justice system were different then and called for other solutions. The response devised in that age was to play a significant part in society's answers to juvenile crime for nearly 130 years afterwards, and laid the foundations for a system that operated until comparatively recently.

In the middle of the nineteenth century, official support was given for the development throughout England and Wales of a range of residential schools offering care, control and education to delinquent children. Over the years this system grew and flourished, despite intermittent difficulties. In the last ten years, however, there has been a dramatic decline in the use of the successors to these schools, the Community Homes with Education (CHE) with the resultant closure of many of them. The reasons for this decline and the manner in which it occurred should not pass unnoticed and unrecorded both because of the importance the schools played in the history of the juvenile justice system and the influence they had on subsequent developments.

The Reformatories and the Industrial Schools and their successors, the Approved Schools and lately the CHEs were spread throughout England and Wales. They housed, in a variety of buildings, many boys and girls and called upon the expertise of teachers, care workers and others. They were, in their time, the direct concern of prominent individuals and institutions from Government Ministers, Magistrates, Police, Churches, Voluntary Agencies to Local Authorities, and concerned people. Although they were at times heralded and feted and at other times pilloried and criticised, they appeared to be part of the fabric of society.

There have been many studies of the schools at various stages in their history (Curtis, 1946; Rose, 1967; Carlebach, 1970; Tutt, 1974; Millham ,1975) but there has been no material that gives a full account of the system up to the present time. This special residential provision is now at its lowest ebb, in terms of demand for its services, staff morale and actual existence, since its inception. There is a definite possibility of the complete demise of these residential schools and that this could pass unchronicled and unexplained. This account aims at ensuring that this is not the case.

As this is primarily an historical study, the methodology used has been in the first instance to consult the relevant data through the literature on the subject and to consider the wealth of official documentation, child care legislation and publications by the associated professional associations. Where information has not been available or adequate a partial survey of local authorities and of former Community Homes with Education (CHE) staff has been undertaken, including conversations with some of the significant people who were involved. These included John Gittins, Principal of Aycliffe, Classifying and Training School (1942-1979) and President of the Heads and Matrons of Approved Schools Association (1968-69), Barbara Kahan, Children's Officer in Oxfordshire during the 1960s and Deputy Chief Social Work Services Officer at the Department of Health and Social Security from 1970 to 1980; Joan Cooper, Chief Inspector at the Home Office Children's Department from 1965-1976; and Haydn Davies Jones, at one time Captain of the Wellesley Nautical Approved School and for many years Senior Lecturer at the University of Newcastle upon Tyne and coordinator of an advanced course for senior staff in the CHEs from its inception in 1961 until the close of the course in 1987.

Among the key issues that have concerned the Schools from their formal beginnings in 1854 until the present have been matters of cost, success and efficiency, management (both local and national), juvenile delinquency and child care legislation.

Often the interaction of these factors, as well as of external influences, produced crises and changes within the system. Thus, for example, cost has always been a major consideration and led in the early days of the Reformatories and Industrial Schools to pressures to economise by using inmates to produce saleable goods and by filling as many of the places in a school as possible. In the 1980s cost was a significant factor in the closure of many schools. It has not always, however been dominant. The need to contain juvenile delinquency in a way that reduced the exposure of young people to the influences of hardened adult offenders has remained the main inspiration for the Schools. A further concern has been the desire to develop an effective system that would have a long term impact on the residents. This led to a constant preoccupation with a measure of efficacy, known as the success rate, in which a young person discharged from the Schools was deemed to have been a success if he or she had not reoffended within three years of discharge.

These various concerns have also been reflected in the legislation affecting children. Thus the Youthful Offenders Act, 1854 was the first important step in recognising that child delinquents and adult offenders should be dealt with in different ways, and the Children and Young Persons Act, 1969 aimed at reducing the stigma of criminality on young offenders. Latterly the Children Act, 1989 and the Criminal Justice Act, 1991 have reverted to the division of care and welfare.

Recent documentary material examined includes a series of Reports of the Department of Health and Social Security Development Group on Community Homes with Education and data from several of the Regional Planning Committees, which were responsible for the coordination of special (and other) children's services.

Forty Local Authority and Voluntary Bodies were surveyed to establish the extent of the decline of the CHE provision in their areas and to ascertain the reasons for this. Seventeen individual accounts of closure, four of these in depth, were obtained in order to illustrate more fully the impact of closure on those involved, including staff and children, and on provision for juvenile delinquents in the areas formerly served by the CHEs. Alternative uses of the redundant buildings has been recorded to indicate how final, in most cases, has been their loss to the child care services.

Seven major areas are explored:

1. The foundation and development of a separate residential care and education service for young offenders and the 'wayward', 1815-1933.
2. The emergence and development of the Approved Schools system, 1933-1969.
3. The changing attitudes towards juvenile delinquency and the subsequent reforming of the law in respect of children and young people, 1960-1975.
4. The transition of the Approved School system to the Community Home with Education, 1969-1980.
5. The development of a philosophy and practice supporting alternative measures to the use of residential care and education for young offenders, 1975-1990.
6. An account of the sharp reduction in the number of CHEs, detailed accounts of the processes of closure in a number of establishments and the impact of closures on those directly involved, 1980-1989.
7. Some consideration of the probable effects of the closures on the future management of young offenders.

The closure of CHEs continues even as this book is being written. The dramatic reduction in their number in the last ten years has not been simply the phased replacement of a system considered to be outdated by a modern well planned alternative. The CHEs have been part of a complex system of interacting features. These included evolving philosophies of child care and education, changing structures in local government and in legislation in respect of children, and hardening attitudes to public expenditure and the financing of welfare provision.

This account strives to be more than a simple chronicle of events, rather it attempts to describe the changing role of a service which was formed in answer to the social malaise of juvenile delinquency. It aims also at clarifying some of the issues that needed to be addressed in that process. It records how the CHE system and its forerunners, played a major part in the response to juvenile offending. It suggests how the achievements and failings of this system may be used as a referral point for those concerned to develop a humane and realistic juvenile justice system. Finally it is hoped that before CHEs are confined to the history books that the role for residential care and education in the care and treatment of young offenders will not go unrecognised.

One

Children in Prison

In February 1814, at the Old Bailey Sessions, five children were condemned to death: two were aged twelve, one aged eleven, one was nine and one aged only eight; they had all been found guilty of burglary in a dwelling. Children could also be sentenced to transportation to the Colonies. The Register of Stafford prison shows, for example, that in 1834 a William Biglen, aged 14 years, was sentenced to transportation for seven years for stealing a silk handkerchief. Matilda Seymour, aged ten years, received a similar sentence for stealing a shawl and a petticoat.

Many children were accommodated in hulks while awaiting transportation. These were old ships lying in the River Thames, the Medway and at Portsmouth. It was said of the hulks that 'of all places of confinement that British history records, they were apparently the most brutalising, the most demoralising and the most horrible. The death rate was appallingly high, even for the prisons of the period' (Pinchbeck and Hewitt, 1973).

In 1815 concern about this cruel and harsh treatment of young delinquents inspired the formation of a group, the Society for Investigating the Causes of the Alarming Increase in Juvenile Delinquency in the Metropolis. The prime aim of this body was to consider other more humane methods of responding to the problem. In the course of its enquiries it had come across very few children who could not be led to amend their delinquent ways by the use of more enlightened treatment. It argued that:

> ...if the degree of punishment were proportioned to the nature of the offence, if the operation of that punishment were uniform and certain, if during confinement they (the offenders), were not exposed to the temptation of idle hours and corrupt society - if the infliction of bodily punishment were to give way to mildness of persuasion and gentleness of reproof - if appeals were oftener made to the moral sensibilities of these youths; and exertions

were made to raise rather than degrade them in their own
estimation the number of juvenile depredators would materially
diminish and the conductors of public prisons would frequently
enjoy the unspeakable felicity of turning the culprit from the
error of his ways (cited by Pinchbeck and Hewitt, 1973).

A grou[...]ly as
1788 to fo[...]ntion
of Vice a[...]up a
number o[...]rried
couple wit[...]could
be engage[...], The
Duke of L[...]came
known as[...]

In 1806[...]shing
The Phila[...]this
Society a[...]the
Alarming[...]polis
was that[...]rned
with mak[...]t the
latter paid[...]ation
of the law[...]neral
provision[...]

A new[...] the
Causes of the Alarming Increase in Juvenile Delinquency in
the Metropolis; this was known by the almost equally wordy
title of 'The Society for The Improvement of Prison Discipline
and for the Reformation of Juvenile Offenders'. This body
undertook a detailed study of the effects of contemporary
prison conditions on the young people committed to them, and
undertook to make extensive visits to the special juvenile
prisons and reformatories already established on the
Continent. The leading member of this Society was Peter
Bedford. One of the results of the deliberations of this group
was that a Bill was introduced into Parliament in 1821 to
make some separate provision for young offenders. This was
the first attempt to introduce legislation specifically concerned
with juvenile delinquents. It was to fail, however, as were a
number of subsequent attempts to introduce separate
measures, until 1847.

There had been some acceptance of the need for separate
penal provision for young offenders in 1823, with the decision

[handwritten note: Penal policy or juveniles. not often considered. distinction from adults. not in fact separate provision until mid 1800s considered.]

to use the hulk *Bellerophon* at Sheerness for 320 boys. This was replaced in 1825 by another hulk, the *Euryalus* stationed at Chatham.

A Select Committee on 'The Police in the Metropolis' included in its report a detailed description of life on the *Euryalus*. It pointed to a daily routine of crushing monotony, rigid discipline and cynical religiosity, in which there was virtually no scope for reformation. The Select Committee advocated a separate prison or a juvenile convict ship for boys. It also recommended the use of special institutions for the destitute.

By 1840 it is possible to identify two main approaches to the reforming of the penal system in regard to juveniles; one advocated the establishment of separate juvenile prisons, the other, educational and home-like reformatories. The emerging reformatory movement was influenced and animated by the example of a number of establishments earlier developed on the Continent. The two most significant of these were Rauhe Haus near Hamburg and La Colonie Agricole at Mettrai. Rauhe Haus was begun by Emmanuel Wicherm and his mother acquiring a small cottage and an acre of land. They took into the cottage fourteen delinquent boys aged between 5 and 18 years. The boys were set to work with the couple to improve the farm, Wicherm and his mother adopting a parental role towards them. The size of the venture grew so that they eventually opened four cottages for boys and two for girls. There were also workshops, a chapel, a washing and drying house and a bake house. 'In this way a home and industrial school was substituted for prison for convicted juveniles' (Heywood, 1965).

La Colonie Agricole was founded at Mettrai near Tours in 1840. The founder, Demetz, based it on the work done at Rauhe Haus. It was, however, on a much larger scale than the earlier project, with provision for 400 boys, grouped into families of 40, cared for by a master and two assistant masters, in each house. The boys were given trade training and a basic education and also given some share in the management of their house.

In 1846 the committee of the Philanthropic Society asked its resident chaplain, the Reverend Sydney Turner, to visit the Colonie Agricole. Turner was determined to adopt a systematic approach to the structuring of the Philanthropic Society. On his return he noted that although there was no possibility of transplanting the ideas and ideals of La Colonie Agricole in

England there were important lessons to be learned from the visit. Carlebach (1970) observed that:

> ...*these were first the employment of trained staff, second the division of the inmates into family groups living in a homely setting; third to act on boys by persuasion rather than force; fourth to give the boys active outdoor occupation such as gardening and agriculture and fifth to combine the charity of individuals with support and sanction of Government.*

In 1849 the Philanthropic Society was transferred from London to Redhill to establish an agricultural colony. There were two houses for boys and staff, later increased to five. On 30th April, Prince Albert laid the foundation stone of the Chapel. The move to Redhill confirmed the Philanthropic Society as a resource exclusively for delinquent boys. In little more than half a century the Philanthropic Society had gradually changed from a voluntary organisation with a rather diffuse concept of rescue and reform of the young to a specialised organisation bent on the rehabilitation of delinquent boys.

While Sydney Turner was adapting his Mettrai experiences to the needs of delinquent boys in England, another notable child care pioneer, Mary Carpenter, was also drawing inspiration for her work from Continental models. She was an energetic campaigner for destitute and delinquent children, writing two books about her methods (Carpenter, 1851; 1853). Carpenter urged that magistrates should have the power to commit convicted children to specially designated schools, should have the power to detain them, and that these schools be supported by Government inspection and grants. She stated that payments for maintenance of the children should be made from the rates or by the parents. Carpenter decided to establish her own Reformatory School and in 1852 opened a mixed sex school at Kingswood, at that time a village just outside of Bristol. Her fundamental belief was that the delinquent child could be changed for the better. She wrote that:

> ...*faith in those around him being once thoroughly established, he will soon yield his own will in ready submission to those who are working for his good; it will thus be gradually subdued and trained, and he will work with them in effecting his reformation, trusting, where he cannot perceive the reasons of the measures they adopt to correct or eradicate the evil in him (Carpenter, 1853).*

Mary Carpenter, joined by a group of like minded people, was now lobbying Parliament for a major restructuring of the penal system to deal with the juvenile delinquent. Among the most notable of her supporters was Matthew Davenport Hill, who was particularly impressed by the system in operation in the County where he was working, Warwickshire, for dealing with first offenders. This was a policy of returning the first time offender to the care of his or her parents and employer on 'probation'. When, as often would be the case, the offender had no family or friend to take this responsibility the magistrates would send the child to an Asylum at Stretton-on-Dunsmore, which they had financed out of their own pockets and from public subscriptions. When Davenport Hill became Recorder of Birmingham in 1839, he became a strong advocate of the 'Warwickshire Plan' which was later adopted in several other parts of the country. Meanwhile in London, Charles Pearson, a distinguished city solicitor proposed that 'special asylums for the criminal and destitute children, in place of ordinary prisons, should be maintained and directed by the State' (Pinchbeck and Hewitt, 1973).

As a direct result of the continuing pressure of this group of active campaigners a Member of Parliament, Adderley (later Lord Norton), moved a motion in the Commons for a Committee to enquire into the treatment of criminal and destitute juveniles. This Committee presented its Report in 1853 and supported many of the ideas of the reformers. A conference was called by the group in November 1853, at which various suggestions were incorporated into a Bill which Adderley introduced into the next session of Parliament under the title of the Youthful Offenders Act which, in amended form, became law in 1854.

Under the Act of 1854 voluntary societies were authorised to provide Reformatory Schools and were given powers to detain offenders under the age of 16 years for between two and five years. The Home Secretary could order a discharge at any time and could transfer offenders from one school to another. He would certify which schools were satisfactory and could withdraw certification if he thought schools or their managers were failing to maintain correct standards. Each School had to be governed by a board of managers. Wherever possible parents were required to make a financial contribution to the upkeep of their child.

Although the Act was aimed primarily at substituting reformatory treatment for retributive punishment, a concession was made to the older principle by including a clause under which children had to serve a 14 day period of imprisonment as an expiation for their crime before they were remitted to the custody of a Reformatory. This was a perpetuation of the belief that crime must be punished and be seen to be punished. It was also held that a short spell in prison would serve as a warning to children of what would be in store for them should they continue to offend.

The Certified Industrial Schools Act, passed in 1857, allowed voluntary institutions to care for potentially delinquent children. The schools were also eligible to apply for grants from public funds. At first there were some distinct differences between the Industrial Schools and the Reformatories. The Industrial Schools were to be certified by the Committees of the Privy Council on Education and inspected by education staff. Children convicted for vagrancy could be placed in an Industrial School but first the justices had to enquire if the parents would provide a surety for the child's good behaviour and only if they could not would an order be made. Children between the ages of 7 and 14 years could be committed and, whatever the age of committal, be retained until the age of 15 years , but the justices could discharge a child at any time on the application of the parents or the managers of the school. The managers could board him out (Rose, 1967).

The Industrial Schools were intended by their founders, most notable of whom was Mary Carpenter, to be places where children were diverted from delinquency either before they had become offenders or whilst they were only minor offenders. They were therefore not initially seen as part of the resources of the Courts. In time, however, the limited measures which enabled Courts to make Orders for placement in an Industrial School led to a close association between the Industrial School and the Reformatories.

In 1860 the responsibility for Industrial Schools was transferred from the Committee of Education to the Home Secretary. Later, in 1866, it became necessary for any proposed modification of school buildings to be approved by the Home Office. The Home Office could withdraw certification and the schools were subject to regular inspection by Home Office officials.

The minimum age for sending children to the Reformatory School was fixed at ten years. The ages of those referred to Industrial Schools varied. All those under 12 years of age found guilty of begging, wandering, being destitute or frequenting the company of reputed thieves were liable for placement in an Industrial School; also all those under 14 years of age who were found, on the application of a parent, to be beyond control.

Many of the administrative and legal structures for the Schools were established in the 12 years between 1854 and 1866. At the same time both the number of schools and the number of children committed to them expanded steadily; by the end of 1865 there were 65 Reformatory and 50 Industrial Schools in Great Britain accommodating 4,915 and 2,062 children respectively. By 1875 the number of Industrial Schools had risen to 117 although the number of Reformatories remained the same. The number of Industrial Schools continued to increase steadily and there were over 15,000 children in such establishments in 1880. In contrast, over the same period the number of Reformatory Schools declined slightly and their population remained at 5,000 to 6,000 children (Rose, 1967).

The rapid growth of the Industrial Schools reflected the increased awareness of those concerned with the welfare of children (whether it was the local Boards of Guardians, the Police or the voluntary child welfare bodies), of the need to make better provision and preparation for employment. These measures in turn helped reduce the number of children taken to the Courts for offending. The humanitarian ideas of some of the early founders of the Reformatory Schools were however often diminished or even lost as the numbers of schools expanded. The discipline in many reformatories was very restrictive; some schools had barred windows and locked doors and insisted that residents had cropped hair. These outward signs of control and regimentation were a reflection of the fact that many of those who were employed in the Reformatories came from the punitive tradition deeply ingrained in society.

A major influence on the management and character of the schools was to be the Home Office Inspectorate. This was established in 1857 as a new department to inspect Reformatory (and later Industrial) Schools and to collect payments from parents. The inspector examined the schools two or three times a year and published an annual report in which he gave findings in general terms. He then described each school under the headings of health, discipline, training, staff cost for the year and results on discharge.

From 1857 to 1911 the Home Office published annual reports based on those of the inspectors. Despite the wide powers of the Home Office it would appear that these powers were rarely used. Control, however, was exercised, mainly in the area of finance. Much emphasis was put on the need for establishments to be managed as economically as possible. This led to an increasing emphasis on the need for the work, originally instituted for the training of residents, to be profitable. Other areas where economies were made included food, clothing and the fabric of the building. A number of establishments tried to qualify for a higher government allowance by admitting more children, some of whom for reasons of age, health or handicap should not have been in the schools.

Although initially the schools relied considerably on voluntary contributions they came to depend, within a relatively short period, almost entirely on Government finance. This is clear from observing the way in which costs were met. In 1860 the total cost of the reformatories was £92,854-5s-6d, of which £24,903-6s-7d was contributed by voluntary subscriptions. In 1880 the total cost was £134,079-16s-8d, of which £5,005-0s-4d was from voluntary subscription. In 1880 public funds provided 90% of the costs of the schools, private subscription 7% and parents and inmates 3% (Carlebach, 1970).

Another important early influence on the Reformatories was the concern felt by some that the young offenders were, by their delinquency, gaining the advantage of a training and education denied at that time to 'ordinary' children. The managers of Reformatories were, in general, acutely conscious of this difficulty and endeavoured to provide these facilities in a way that was unlikely to be agreeable to the young offender. As a result the education provided was poor in quality, and the work hard.

The Schools seemed to have achieved their objectives of curbing delinquency. A close watch was kept on the 'success rate' of the schools. 'Success' was considered to have been achieved when a child had not been reconvicted within three years of his or her discharge.

The general impact of the Reformatory and Industrial Schools in their first 30 years was considerable. They are credited with having broken up the gangs of young criminals in the large towns, with putting an end to the training of boys as professional thieves, and with rescuing children fallen into crime from becoming hardened offenders. Thus the schools clearly had an effect in preventing large numbers of children entering a life of crime. These conclusions are recorded in the report of the Reformatory and Industrial Schools Commission of 1884. The statistics showed that the commitment of juveniles to prison in England and Wales fell from 13,981 in 1856 to 7,138 in 1876, and to 5,483 in 1881.

Acquiring the 3 Rs
(The Royal Philanthropic School in the 1890s)

The boys band - developing talent and discipline
(The Royal Philanthropic School in the 1890s)

Two

Conflicting Aims

Although the Reformatories and the Industrial Schools were clearly intended for delinquent or near delinquent children their existence and development should be seen in the broader context of the total provision made for 'problem' children or children with a need for care outside the confines of their families. All were vulnerable and their categorisation was often dependent on whichever of the arms of society they initially fell into, for example the police, education authorities, voluntary organisations, or the 'Parish'.

In the early days following the Poor Law Act of 1834 many children went into the workhouse with their destitute parents. It is reported that in 1840 there were 64,570 children in workhouses. It soon became apparent that the Poor Law was not having a major impact on the number of children needing alternative care. A number of voluntary bodies sprang up to support, and eventually largely take over, the task of caring for these children. Much of this work was based on the concern of various religious denominations for the spiritual as well as the physical welfare of children.

The 'cottage home' type of residential care, developed from the ideas of Mettrai and Rauhe Haus referred to earlier, was established by some of the founders of the voluntary organisations. The best known example was Dr Barnardos Village Home for Girls, opened at Barkingside in 1876. Another provision, which became much favoured following the Children Act 1948, was the system of scattered homes. This idea was pioneered by the Sheffield Board of Guardians in 1896. They opened nine ordinary houses scattered in working class areas. These were intended to be indistinguishable from other houses in the areas in which they were located (Heywood, 1965).

A system of caring for children who were unable to live with their own families but which did not involve residential care was 'boarding out' or the placing of children from an institution with families in the community. This idea was supported by

Florence Davenport Hill as early as 1868. She argued that boarding out could be a highly efficient method of caring for children, that it was cheaper than any other method and that 'it made for a greater happiness of children than any other method of dealing with children on the rates'.

There was some resistance to the idea of boarding out. In the first place there were objections because of the need to work across the boundaries of the Poor Law authorities. Secondly there was a fear that boarding out would give pauper children a lifestyle above that to which they were used and so 'a reward will be given to improvidence and a stimulus given to immorality' (Henry Fawcett, 1881, as cited by Pinchbeck and Hewitt, 1973). Despite these fears, the practice slowly became an accepted option. In 1885 an Association for the Advancement of Boarding Out was formed to forward its cause. The Local Government Board, which replaced the Poor Law Board, issued an Order regulating boarding out in 1877. By 1885 the Unions who managed the Poor Law were between them boarding out 2,799 children and by 1895 5,572 children. The voluntary child care organisations were very actively committed to the idea of boarding out. The Waifs and Strays Society boarded out many of its children. Barnardo was also in favour of the practice and by 1896 he was boarding out more children than all the Poor Law authorities of the country.

Whilst these alternative types of child care were developing, ideas and concerns about the manner in which the Reformatory and Industrial Schools were progressing led to Parliament appointing the Reformatory and Industrial Schools Commission in 1883. The Commission was the result of public unease about conditions in the schools and also of the continuing debate about the practice of the 14 day imprisonment clause in the Youthful Offenders Act 1854. The specific brief of the Commission was 'to enquire and report upon the operation, management, control, inspection, financial arrangements and conditions generally of certified Reformatories'.

The Commission supported the view that there should be some form of short sharp punishment before placement in the Reformatory. It declared that in most cases this would continue to take the form of imprisonment but, for boys under the age of 14 years, recommended that magistrates should have the alternative of ordering them to be whipped at the Police station. It was suggested that girls have a period of solitary confinement - seven days for those aged under 12 years, 14 days for those aged 12 years and upwards.

The Commission urged that there should be more women managers, especially for girls schools and thought schools should either be small or divided into small units. They also urged that all non-educational industries should be abolished, that the profit motive in children's work should be eliminated, that education should be given more importance and be improved, and that the schools should be inspected more frequently.

Education had remained a source of contention throughout the history of the Reformatory Schools and their successors. The Commission noted that:

The teachers employed are frequently insufficient in number, and of inferior quality, although a strong and highly qualified teaching staff is needed in consequence of the inferiority of the material ... and the methods and appliances of the school are often antiquated and second rate and do not come up to the requirements of the Education Department in public elementary schools.

The Reformatory and Industrial Schools Commission considered that it should be the duty of the Education Department to inspect the Schools but would not support the idea of transferring responsibility of the Reformatory Schools to the Education Department.

The Commission made recommendations limiting the terms of residence in a Reformatory from three to five years for younger or first time offenders; they required that managers should state in writing their reasons for refusing a request for admission of a child; they made proposals to limit the use of punishment; and made recommendations for the establishment of special Reformatories for 'refractory cases'. They urged greater use of the release of children on licence; and recommended the building of more halfway hostels.

The debate on the desirability of requiring the young offender to serve a short term of imprisonment before admission to the Reformatory was not ended by the 1884 Commission. This and other related issues continued to be of concern until a later Committee resolved this matter and advanced a number of other ideas. The later Committee reported in 1896 and was far more radical than its predecessor. There were an unusually large number of minority reports by members, with nine memoranda added to the main report. The Committee was not only concerned with immediate matters but also with the principles underlying practice in the Schools.

Consideration was given to the issue of the criteria to be used, beyond that of criminality, for placing a child in a residential setting. The majority of members concluded that children should not generally be removed from their home unless it was clear that the home and the circumstances required it, and that the value of the placement to the child later in life should be taken into account.

The Committee voiced concern about the influence on a child of living in residence with other, perhaps more hardened delinquents. They looked to the schools as being 'primarily instruments for offering children a happy and constructive environment'. This was a fundamentally different way of viewing the purpose and value of the Reform School system. Prior to this the emphasis of the system had been primarily on the need to protect the community from the young offender, whose own needs were seen very much as a secondary consideration.

Two of the practical results of this approach were the recommendations by the Committee to abolish the requirement for a child to serve a preliminary period of imprisonment and to urge that the Reform and Industrial Schools should be treated as one service. The former proposal was accepted and later incorporated into the Reformatory Schools Act 1899. The latter did not meet with a general welcome at the time but was significant in that it pointed out the difficulty of distinguishing between the delinquent and the disordered, a dilemma which has remained until the present time.

The whole concept of institutional care for the delinquent or the predelinquent child also began to be challenged at the end of the nineteenth century. The annual report of the Howard Association published in 1896 commented on 'an institution craze' that had 'taken hold of the public fancy', and according to a letter in *The Times* in 1899 'most of us are losing faith ... by herds and battalions in the Reformatory Schools'.

Probation was introduced in a limited form by the Probation of First Offenders Act 1887. This did little more than allow convicted first offenders to return home to their families.

Supervision of those on Probation was eventually included in the Probation Act of 1907.

The main reasons for the many Government enquiries over such a short period were primarily to improve the financial management and governmental control of the Reformatory Schools. The Treasury was concerned about the increasing expenditure needed while the schools found themselves in a series of financial crises. Behind these difficulties remained the ever present problems of how to provide a satisfactory service of high quality through a series of semi-independent units imperfectly controlled from the centre. Despite these conflicting demands on the schools a belief in their intrinsic worth ensured their continued existence.

The Youthful Offenders Act 1901 was a further reflection of the changing attitudes towards the young offender. It allowed for a child or young person to be held on remand in a place other than prison and extended the powers of committal to an Industrial School rather than to a prison.

A major advance in child care legislation was heralded with the introduction of The Children Act 1908, popularly known as 'The Children's Charter'. The Act was designed to consolidate the legislation dealing with the protection of children and the training and treatment of child offenders. As well as being a 'tidying up' Act, it introduced a clear system for the management of children who came within the purview of the judicial system. It also required the police to provide places of detention for juveniles remanded in custody.

The most radical part of the Act was the introduction of Juvenile Courts. These were to deal exclusively with matters concerning children and young people, offenders and non-offenders. The Courts had to be held in a separate room and at a separate time from those dealing with adult offenders and the public were not to be admitted to them. Parents were required to attend the Court and to pay fines for the children's offences. Children were to be dealt with in accordance with their needs not simply punished for their offences.

Any child could be sent to a Reformatory School if convicted of an offence punishable in an adult with imprisonment, and be detained for a period of between three and five years up to the age of 19 years, whichever was the soonest.

Any child under 14 years of age could be sent to an Industrial School if found to be begging, wandering or destitute; in the care of parents with drunken habits; as could the daughter of a father convicted of sexual assaults on her; frequenting the company of thieves or prostitutes; failing to attend school, refractory in the workhouse, or beyond control.

A child could be detained for as long a period of time as the Court directed, but not beyond the age of 16 years. Reformatory School leavers were to remain under supervision until 19 years of age, and Industrial School leavers until 18 years of age. The managers could allow children to leave the school after they had been resident for 18 months but they remained subject to recall to complete their full term if they reoffended Such children were said to be released on licence. Transfers between Reform and Industrial Schools were made possible but only on the specific authority of the Secretary of State. The local education authority was required to make payments for children in Industrial Schools and Reformatories, and were to receive payments from other local authorities who placed children in the schools. Although these changes were generally seen as a response to the problems of childhood delinquency there was still concern about the regimes of many Reformatories.

This came to a head in a report of several occurrences at one particular school, the Akbar Nautical Training School, in 1910. In the magazine *John Bull* it was alleged by the Deputy Superintendent and Matron that such severe punishments were inflicted on the boys that some had subsequently died as a result. The Government eventually conducted an enquiry into the allegations but concluded there had been no brutality although some irregular punishments had taken place. These findings were thought by *John Bull* to be largely a 'whitewashing' of the true events. The system however rallied round to support those in authority. As Carlebach (1970) observed: 'It was a case of which comes first, the schools or the children. Following this incident the public argued for the children first, whilst the schools opted for the protection of the system'.

The schools were also vulnerable to attack by those who felt that they were not structured and punitive enough. In September 1911 the *Daily Mail* ran a series of articles called 'Schools for Crime'. Amongst their allegations was one that the boys lacked proper supervision. As a result of this continued concern, and particularly of the Akbar affair, a committee was set up by the Home Office to enquire into the constitution, management, discipline and education in Reformatory and Industrial schools.

The Committee reported that, in 1911, there were 37 Reformatories, none of which were run by local authorities and 112 Industrial Schools, of which 22 were with local authorities. The main thrust of the recommendations was for an increase in the control and inspection powers of the Home Office and for a special branch of the Home Office to be formed to deal with children, the certified schools and the juvenile courts. The Report was also concerned with improving the quality of senior and of teaching staff, noting that although the number of certificated teaching staff in the schools had risen from 151 in 1896 to 228 in 1913, there were still 47 schools without any certified teachers. There were also recommendations to improve the medical care of the children, the systems of discipline and punishments, industrial training, leisure activities and domestic arrangements.

Although there were some improvements following this Report many of the problems remained unresolved, particularly in respect of the control and financing of the system. Local authorities were particularly dissatisfied with the fees charged by the schools, fees which varied immensely from one school to another. In 1919 the Home Office supplied what was a generally acceptable solution to this problem - there would be a flat rate per child, calculated upon the total estimated cost, half to be paid by the local authority responsible for the child and half by the Home Office.

The schools (both Reformatory and Industrial) reached their peak of occupancy in 1912 with a total population of 25,752 children resident in 44 Reformatories and 116 Industrial Schools. By 1926 however there were only 28 Reformatories and 56 Industrial Schools with a total population of 6871. This was indeed a dramatic decline. Heywood (1965) noted that between 1915 and 1925 committals of boys to Reformatories were halved and committals to Industrial Schools fell by an even larger proportion. The more difficult type of child was sent to the Home Office schools, the less difficult were usually placed on probation or dealt with by fines or binding over.

These developments were the result of many factors. Sidney Haris, Head of the Children's Department in 1924, suggested four factors: the reluctance of local authorities to pay; the impact of probation; the unemployment situation which kept families at home together; and the improved educational system.

Two other factors, noted by Rose (1967) were the general decline in juvenile delinquency and the change in attitude to the Reformatories from the nineteenth century view that they were necessary and generally constructive alternatives to prison to the belief that young people should not be committed to any institution if this was avoidable.

The staff and managers of the schools through their respective powerful and influential Associations, complained forcefully about the considerable decline in the use of the Schools. They pointed in particular to the very high success rates for the Schools, rates of between 85 and 90%, as outlined in the Report of the Departmental Commission on the Treatment of Young Offenders, published by HMSO in 1927.

Continued concern about the role of the Schools and the law dealing with children and young offenders led to the appointment of a new Departmental Committee in 1925. Reporting in 1929 it recommended that the Reformatory and Industrial Schools should be merged into one system of schools 'approved' by the Home Office - thus the title, Approved Schools These schools would provide short term training to enable boys and girls to take their place as happy and useful citizens in society.

It was recommended that the minimum age of committal be raised to 10 years of age and a maximum period of three years residence be adopted. Managers were no longer to be allowed to refuse a request for admission. The Committee made many recommendations on the use of Borstal institutions for young people. All these recommendations were incorporated in the Children and Young Persons Act 1933.

The legislation was far reaching in its effects. Under the 1933 Act a child was defined as someone up to the age of 14 years and a young person as someone between 14 and 17 years of age. The statute laid down specifications for the composition of the juvenile court panel. Education authorities were required to provide magistrates with information about the family and the school record of children appearing in Court. The Act made clearer the scope and function of places of detention for children on remand and introduced Remand Homes. It allowed for children in need of care and protection, because they were beyond control of their parents, to be placed under the supervision of a probation officer or be subject to a Fit Person Order, rather than be sent to an Approved School. While the Home Office retained responsibility for the management of Approved Schools and child care issues in general at local level, the care of the children was to be the responsibility of the local education committee.

In the view of Heywood (1965) the Children and Young Persons Act 1933 was especially significant in that it heralded a move away from the idea that neglected and delinquent children were social failures needing to purge themselves by hard work - 'The welfare of the child, and not the judgement of society, was now paramount'. There was however little heed given to any ideas of rehabilitation to the family. Instead it was considered right and prudent that the child be removed from ineffectual parents and placed either in the care of a 'fit person' or in a children's home or Approved School.

Many of the strengths and weaknesses of the Industrial and Reformatory Schools system were to be carried forward into the new Approved School system. The management of the schools by local personages had much to commend it, although in practice this often led to a conventional approach and to ossified views. Its strengths were that it involved interested local people who were prepared to take on responsibilities that no public body was empowered to undertake. The main weakness of this system of management was that it was accountable to an often distant central government department, the Home Office.

The managers were self appointed people whose own lifestyle was often far removed from that of the young people over whom they had responsibility and whose knowledge of institutional life was based substantially on their own experiences, usually of public school and/or the armed forces. Yet, for the most part, the strengths of the arrangement seemed to outweigh its weaknesses.

There was, from the start, a degree of contradiction in the schools attitude to parents. On the one hand it was usually the case that the schools saw themselves as preparing young people for separate and independent lives from their families, while on the other they saw the parents as having a responsibility to make a contribution to the upkeep of their children. This latter practice was largely explained by the persistent fear that if parents were not made to pay a contribution they would simply opt out altogether of any responsibility for bringing up their children. The actual amount paid by parents was an insignificant part of the total cost and the system rapidly became dependent on central and local government finance.

Finance played an important part in the whole system of certified schools: there was constant pressure to keep costs down and this led to abuses such as giving the young people tasks designed to raise income rather than preparing them for employment and admitting more children than the school was authorised to contain. Financial considerations also placed limits on the number and quality of staff engaged , including teachers. This together with the concern that the children should not be better educated than the non-delinquent children of poor families, ensured that the quality of formal education in the schools remained low. A degree of central government funding and the emergence of the schools as a statutory resource for the Juvenile Courts resulted in them continuing to be an integral part of a State sponsored system.

A further important component of the system, related in part to the 'value for money' concept and in part to the wish to measure effectiveness was the recording of the 'success rate'. From the beginning of the schools up until 1933 the published figures showed that they had been effective in these respects. When, in later years, the results were not nearly so favourable, doubts began to be expressed about the validity of this method of measurement.

At the beginning of the certified school system the range of alternative provision in this field was limited. Later, with the growth of different options together with the changes in society, such as the trend towards smaller families, relatively less poverty, and universal education, gradually the demand for the services offered by the schools diminished. Nevertheless in 1933 the newly created 'Approved Schools' system was an integral part of the juvenile justice system. It inherited many of the structures created by its forerunners including methods of finance, inspection and management. With its range of buildings, staff and management structures, the Approved Schools were to continue to be a major resource of the state in its response to juvenile delinquency.

Three

The Formation of the Approved Schools

A *Handbook for Managers of Approved Schools* (Home Office Children's Department, 1961) stated that the aims and function of the Approved School training were:

> *...education (in the formal sense), religious education and guidance, practical or vocational training, attention to health and to the use of recreation, social training (how to live with others) and personal case-work (help with personal problems).*

These functions were directed to achieving the aims of the re-adjustment and social re-education of the boys and girls in preparation for their rehabilitation into the community. The Reynolds Report (Reynolds, 1946) into pay and conditions in the Approved Schools suggested that the merits of the system were that, by membership of a small group within the context of the larger group, the child would learn to have status and respect for the rights of others. It went on to argue that, in the larger group, there would be opportunities for freedom in activities during leisure time and instruction to equip the child for employment which would preserve self respect and encourage self-reliance.

The extent of the magnitude of the task undertaken by the Approved Schools was fully recognised and explained in a later government enquiry into the management of young offenders, the 'Ingleby Report' (Ingleby, 1960). This Report found that children admitted to the schools often had a long history of difficult and anti-social behaviour and that many had been subject to other forms of treatment which had failed. Some children were also retarded in their education and had suffered from emotional disturbances, many had been removed from broken or inadequate homes to which they still retained loyalty. There were said to be special problems presented by adolescent girls and by the apparently increasing proportion of more difficult and undisciplined boys. Despite what Ingleby called 'such unpromising material' the degree of success was thought to be encouraging.

At the time of the merger of the Industrial Schools and the Reformatories in 1933-34 there were 86 establishments, the majority being former Industrial Schools. By 1938 there were 104 Approved Schools containing 7,268 boys and 1,496 girls. The majority of the new schools, rising from 18 in 1933 to 31 by 1938, were for girls.

Until the mid 1950s the average number of places in a boys school was 100, with a few schools having up to 150 places but very rarely more than this. Some schools for boys offered only 50 places. Schools for girls were much smaller, with an average of 35 places. The range of properties used to accommodate the Approved Schools was considerable. The official handbook on the schools, *Making Citizens* , published by HMSO in 1946, observed that 'a child sent to an Approved School today may find himself housed in an army hut or a small cottage, a reconditioned Reformatory, a Georgian mansion, or a neo-Gothic castle'. The schools were not systematically planned and often found themselves in the buildings they occupied almost by chance. The Curtis Committee considered that many of the buildings used as Approved Schools were handicapped to some extent because they had seldom been constructed for their existing function (Curtis, 1946).

The members of the Curtis Committee visited 52 Approved Schools and so were well placed to comment on the state of the service as they found it shortly after World War II. They recorded some detailed descriptions of the schools and these records gave a useful account of the range and type of service then on offer. An example of a senior boys school with 140 places shows that the building had been taken over from the public assistance authorities in 1936. Situated on the fringe of an industrial area overlooking a wide stretch of open country, it had extensive grounds for playing fields and a walled fruit and vegetable garden. The building itself was rather forbidding, made up of large barrack-like blocks with a high surrounding wall. An entry archway and workshops had been added to the building. The living quarters were in one block divided into two identical halves. There was no living room other than a dining room which also served as a recreation room. In the dining room each table was for 10 boys. Each of the dormitories housed 70 boys in four long rows of beds. There were long concrete floored and tiled wall corridors. Effort had been made to brighten the rooms by paint and distemper. The place looked clean and polished.

A contrasting example of an intermediate school for 120 boys described a Jacobean country house set in 36 acres of garden and playing fields. Some of the staff lived in cottages on the estate. The boys living and recreational rooms were excellent. There was a beautiful dining hall with tables seating six children. The entire place was cheerful and attractive, the institutional atmosphere 'being tempered by the architectural beauty and modernisation'.

Some of the schools, especially former Industrial Schools, were situated in or close to urban areas, but the majority were in the country. Since the number of schools increased rapidly during World War II one of the major reasons for this development was the need to site schools in what the Sixth Report of the Children's Committee (Home Office, 1951) called 'the less vulnerable areas'.

Although some Industrial Schools and a few of the Reformatories had at some time in their history been schools for both boys and girls, none of the Approved Schools were mixed sex schools. At the beginning of the new system there were five schools with both boys and girls in them and although they were given certificates of approval, they were not taken into the Home Office system and so never formally became Approved Schools.

Approved Schools were divided into categories, designated according to the age range of children they accommodated. This was to separate the younger delinquent and/or deprived child from the older, possibly more hardened offender and also to provide education for the appropriate age groupings. The gradings for boys were: Junior, up to 13 on admission, Intermediate, between the ages of 13 years of age and 15, and Senior, up to the age of 17 years. Girls schools were, until 1964/ 1965, divided into Junior for girls under 15 of age and Senior for girls over 15 years of age. Latterly, however, Intermediate Schools were provided for girls aged between 14 and 16 years.

The majority of the schools, like their predecessors, were owned by voluntary organisations which had been founded by people with a definite religious commitment. Thus some schools were run by the Church of England and others by nonconformist organisations such as the National Children's Homes, Barnardos or the Salvation Army. There were two schools run by Jewish orientated groups, although very few Jewish children were thought to have been sent to Approved Schools. The Roman Catholics were the most insistent on children of their Faith being sent to their own schools. The Home Office respected and endorsed this belief in the importance of religion in the Approved Schools system.

Each school had its own board of managers: local people of stature selected by the sponsoring agency and by the existing board. No specific number of people were required to make up a board, this was left to each individual school.

The managers were a particularly important group of people in any Approved School as under the terms of the Children and Young Persons Act 1933: '...all rights and powers exercisable by law by a parent in respect of a boy under the care of the managers of an Approved School are vested in the managers'. It was a requirement that some of the managers lived within reasonable distance of the school to ensure close contact and adequate supervision. At least two of the managers of a school for girls had to be men and at least two had to be women at a school for boys. The managers of schools run by Local Authorities were appointed by the Local Authority Children's Committee.

An additional requirement under the terms of the Criminal Justice Act 1961 was that all boards of managers of voluntary run schools had to have at least one local authority representative. The distribution of the management responsibilities for the Schools in 1967 is shown in Figure 1 .

Table 1

Management Bodies with Responsibility for Approved Schools 1967

	Boys	Girls	Total
Independent	44	17	61
National Voluntary	20	12	32
Local Authority	26	4	30

From data provided by Rose, 1967

The Approved School Rules 1933 (amended in 1949) were very specific about the duties of the managers and how these duties were to be carried out. A Finance Committee had to be appointed. The Home Secretary had to be informed of the names of all managers and also of their death or retirement.

Managers were required to meet monthly 'as far as practicable'. Minutes had to be kept and made available to a Home Office Inspector or District Auditor. Managers were urged to pay frequent visits to the school and at least one manager should visit the school each month and enter observations in the school log book. Managers were responsible for exercising effective control over all expenditure. They were also responsible for the appointment, suspension or dismissal of all staff in the school, although the Secretary of State had to confirm the appointment of a Head. The Handbook (Home Office Children's Department, 1961) urged that managers:

...should know, and be known by, as many of the children as possible. It is important that the managers should know the staff and be familiar with their problems and the conditions under which the work of the school is conducted.

The most significant person in the everyday management of an Approved School was the Head. Prior to the 1950s, it was not uncommon for the Headship to be the preserve of a particular family. This often involved other posts, particularly that of Matron. The Approved Schools handbook, *Making Citizens,* published by HMSO in 1946, observed that the post of Matron was a position second only in importance to that of the Headmaster in the opportunities it gave for influencing the boys.

The quality of the staffing in the schools was recognised by the Home Office as an important factor. Concern about this quality prompted the Home Secretary to appoint a Committee (the Reynolds Committee) to examine the issue of remuneration and conditions of service for staffs in Approved Schools. There had been no such review since 1935 and there was anxiety about the poor quality of applicant that was being attracted to the service and the difficulty of retaining able staff.

One of the main reasons for the staffing difficulties of that time was that there had been a rapid increase in the number of Approved Schools during World War II, with the number of children accomodated increasing from 3,913 in 1938 to a peak of 5,973 in 1942. Many of the able bodied men who could have been employed in the schools were serving in the Armed Forces. Reynolds (1946) notes that: '...in many schools the strain had proved too great, especially for new recruits to the staff'.

The complex staffing structure of an Approved School in

1945 (a structure which was to remain until the mid 1960s) was well described in the Reynolds Report (Reynolds, 1946). Schools for boys had the Headmaster, a Deputy Headmaster, Teachers, Housemasters (operating 'experimentally' in only a few schools in 1945), Instructors, Clerks, Welfare Officers, Housemaids or Headmaster's Maid, Cooks, Needlewomen, General Maids, Matron and Assistant Matrons, and, in some schools, Farm Bailiffs. In girls' schools the staffing was made up of the Headmistress, Deputy Headmistress, Staff Matrons (Instructors), Hostel Matrons, and Cottage Mothers (Housemistresses) and Nurses.

Salaries of Heads were calculated on the basis of the recommendations of a sub-committee of the teachers national negotiating committee, known as the Burnham Committee. There were five grades of schools, determined by their size. Accommodation in Approved Schools was counted as double their actual number for the purpose of calculating Heads salaries, with three additional increments added. Teachers were paid an extra three increments above the norm and were allowed a small payment for an average of 15 hours extraneous duties per week.

The post of Housemaster was an innovation. The Reynolds Report defined a Housemaster's main duties as making close individual contact with a group of boys, planning and supervising their leisure time activities. It was proposed that Housemasters should also become involved in after care arrangements. Postholders should be mature men able to obtain a recognised qualification. They were paid the same salary, at that time, as teachers, and were to be given an additional increment for each year aged over 25 years, subject to a maximum starting point of £375 per annum.

The position of Clerk carried important responsibilities, dealing with the bulk of correspondence with the Courts, local authorities and parents and with the management of financial transactions and statistical returns.

The majority of Headmistresses of girls schools were not qualified teachers, unlike the Headmasters in most boys schools. The Committee accepted this observing that the problems that are dealt with in girls schools 'are more often of a social or moral (nature) than an ordinary type'.

While the prospect of a qualified teacher being a Headmistress was welcomed it was accepted that other relevant qualifications, such as social work, might also be appropriate. The Committee also recommended that the posts, in girls schools, of House Matron and Cottage Mother should be designated as Housemistress.

In 1949 there were 1,075 filled teaching posts in the Approved Schools, including 273 Heads and Deputies and 462 Trade Instructors. This resulted in a general staffing ratio of 20 pupils to a teacher, usually with a handicraft teacher in addition. In schools where trade training was given, the standard aimed at was 10 pupils per instructor. The Select Committee on Estimates (Select Committee for Estimates, 1948-49) thought it necessary to record, for the benefit of potential critics, the reason for the apparent generous staffing of Approved Schools. They noted that a child in an Approved School had to be supervised 24 hours a day and that there was no reserve of teachers. Unlike other boarding schools they were open throughout the year and had to be kept running whilst some staff took their holidays.

By 1960 the number of Housemasters and Housemistresses had increased to 240. The teaching staff remained, however, by far the largest group at 910 (this included Heads and Instructors). The population of the 117 schools at that time was 7,770. The ratio of the professional staff was 1 to 8 pupils.

Although salaries for staff were depressed there was a belief that the accommodation that was offered made up for any shortcomings. Reynolds reported, however, that the standard of accommodation was notoriously low even though there had been some progress, and maintained that the lack of proper amenities not only discouraged some applicants from accepting appointments but caused others to resign shortly after appointments had been taken up.

The accommodation provision did improve in the 1960s. The Williams Report (Williams, 1967), which enquired into staffing issues in all forms of residential care, noted that the majority of Heads of Approved Schools expressed themselves satisfied with their own accommodation and that of married staff but were concerned about the position of single staff. It was also noted that half of the care staff were resident in the same building as the children and a further third were resident on the campus but in separate accommodation. It was generally accepted that the professional staff of the Approved Schools had to live in or near the school.

A flat rate was charged for accommodation, one for single quarters and the other for married quarters. Heads and Matrons were given accommodation, and emoluments, completely free of charge because, it was said, their responsibilities ran throughout the 24 hours of the day.

The expectation and general acceptance of the notion that staff would be resident on or near the campus of Approved Schools continued until the introduction of the Community Home Schools in 1972. There were a number of reasons for this. Firstly there were definite financial benefits. Secondly because of the hours of duty it was usually much more convenient to live on the campus. Thirdly there was a belief that, as staff, they were part of the residential community of the Approved School, which meant being readily available in a crisis and often at other times and so adding to the security and support offered to children and colleagues.

The Sixth Report of the Children's Department (Home Office, 1951) recognised that the Reynolds Committee had been of great significance in laying down general principles and specific terms of salaries and conditions. It had related the salaries of teachers, instructors, and Heads to Burnham scales and laid down a requirement for qualifications before a certain salary and status could be achieved. The position of teachers in respect of extraneous duties was clarified and annual leave of eight weeks was agreed.

The new post of Housemaster was introduced, which the Sixth Report called 'the social worker type of staff'. Despite Reynolds wish that housemasters should hold a recognised qualification in practice such people were hard to find. A compromise position was reached whereby the schools managers could appoint an unqualified person to such a post if they had been accepted by the Home Office as suitable for training in due course.

In 1951 separate salary negotiating committees for teachers and instructors and for housemasters were formed. The divergence that grew between these two groups of staff was to contribute to divisions within the Approved School system and weaken its abilities to function effectively. It was also to be a significant distraction from the issue of survival at a later stage.

Opportunities for residential child care staff to undergo training was made a priority by the Home Office and the

Central Training Council in Child Care was given the task of establishing full time training courses. By 1966 there were 14 one year courses in various parts of England and Wales leading to a certificate in the residential care of children, and two Senior Certificate Courses of one year duration, one at the University of Bristol and the other at the University of Newcastle upon Tyne.

Despite these training opportunities and an insistence by the Home Office that all Housemasters and Housemistresses who were appointed had to be suitable to undergo training at a later date, the Williams Report (Williams, 1967) found that only 15% of residential child care staff were qualified, though this figure was slightly higher for staff in Approved Schools.

As the teaching profession was much better established and as, after World War II, all teachers were required to be qualified their pay and conditions of service improved at a much more rapid pace than that of the residential care workers. Cawson (1978) in her study of Community Homes, considered that the eventual consequence of this, and of the parallel development of the social work emphasis in the schools, was that there was a dominant group of professional staff who had been trained to fulfil one set of professional goals and were expected to divert their energy and resources to the fulfilment of completely different ones. She concluded that: 'It seems inevitable that this would create organisational strain'.

Four

Preoccupations of the System

A major concern of the Home Office had been the need to keep the costs of the Schools to the minimum, consistent with good child care. The methods of their financing the system had been established during the earlier time of the Certified Schools. The schools submitted estimates each year, from which was calculated the average cost per child. The Home Office then fixed a rate per child to be paid by the local authority named on the admittance order. This was expected to produce half the total costs, the remainder was made up by the Treasury. The Courts set an amount to be paid by the child's parents, this was not very high and was often difficult and expensive to collect. The responsibility for collection rested with the local authorities who were allowed to retain 10% of the amount to offset expenses.

The Home Office sometimes made grants for major improvements to individual schools, repayable over 20 years. This extra outlay in many schools, together with additional expenditure, in all the schools, for higher and material and professional standards, improved staff salaries, and the general effect of inflation resulted in ever increasing annual costs of Approved Schools (see Table 2 overleaf).

The Ingleby Report (1960) explained the reasons behind the high costs of the Schools - the charges were required to meet year round provision of schoolroom education, vocational training and residential care; the provision of food, clothing, medical attention, leisure activities, pocket money and after care supervision for the children; salaries and superannuation for the staff; maintenance, improvement or extension of premises and all overhead charges. The need to have a high ratio of staff to children further increased costs.

Table 2
Weekly Charges per Child and Annual Cost and Occupancy
Data for All Approved Schools 1951-1965

Year	Weekly Cost	Average No.	Total Cost (£'000)
1951-52	£ 6- 3- 7d	9,156	2,957
1952-53	£ 6- 6- 2d	9,416	3,098
1953-54	£ 6-16-11d	8,930	3,187
1954-55	£ 7-17- 0d	7,912	3,239
1955-56	£ 8-11- 5d	7,122	3,192
1956-57	£ 9- 2- 1d	6,810	3,232
1957-58	£ 9- 0- 0d	7,056	3,496
1958-59	£ 9- 8- 1d	7.615	3,733
1959-60	£ 9-19- 9d	7,912	4,131
1960-61	£11- 9- 9d	7,910	4,523
1961-62	£11-11- 6d	8,241	4,974
1962-63	£13- 4- 3d	8,605	5,928
1963-64	£15- 3- 6d	8,683	6,890
1964-65	£16-13- 5d	8,664	7,532

From Home Office figures as recorded by Rose, 1967

In the early 1960s there was an upsurge in building in order
to bring the living accommodation, educational and recreational
facilities up to a more satisfactory standard. This building
programme was launched on the basis of a projected
expenditure of £5 million over the following five years. By the
end of 1960, building projects of varying sizes were affecting, or
were expected to affect, over 100 of the 117 schools. Some of the
projects were to provide new classrooms, workshops, gymnasia,
and staff accommodation. Others were to improve structures of
buildings or bring heating, sanitation or kitchens up to modern
standards. In many of the Senior and Intermediate boys schools,
separate 'house' units for about 30 boys were erected.

The high costs of Approved Schools had long been a target
for criticism and question by politicians and some sections of
the press. The Association of Headmasters, Headmistresses
and Matrons of Approved Schools were aware of the
vulnerability of their schools to such criticism as is clear from
the comments of the President of the Association in 1959:

From time to time ill-informed spokesmen launch an attack on
the cost of the Approved Schools and the general public are

invited to raise its eyebrows in horror. I have often seen it quoted that a boy can be educated at Eton or Harrow for no more than it costs to detain a boy in an Approved School.

He then went on to observe that the annual Public School fee of from £425 to £450 per annum simply covered board and tuition for 36 weeks in the year. The annual expenditure of £450 for a child in an Approved School included every aspect of the child's life in the School for almost the whole year, hence comparison was invidious. This did not, however, stop such comparisons being made.

Costs continued to rise at a rate well beyond inflation. By 1970/71 the cost per child per week had reached £31 and the total annual costs were just under £12 million. As Gill (1974) observed: 'In a society that prefers to pay by results, there was understandable concern'. This remark was prompted by concern both about the cost of the Schools and declining success rates. These rates recorded how many of the young people discharged from Approved Schools had avoided reconviction in the subsequent three years. Gill pointed out that, until 1954, the success rates had been based on figures made available via the after care services of the school. It was only after that time that the Home Office itself presented the figures in a consistent form (see Table 3 overleaf).

The significance and interpretation of success rate figures were questioned by some. Rose (1967), for example, observed that reconviction was a very inadequate indication of success or failure, taking little account of the amount of after-care support the ex-Approved School young person received or of the seriousness of the committed offence. If absolute and conditional discharges and fines were excluded on the grounds that they suggested minor offences then the success rate for boys placed out in 1959 was 61%, not 43% as suggested by the figures supplied by the Home Office.

Not all children sent to Approved Schools were offenders. This was especially true of girls who were often placed for care and control. As they were not offenders, and usually did not become offenders, the success rate in respect of girls reflected this and remained fairly constant; 81% in 1933, 84% in 1956. Nevertheless, the Schools were generally perceived as dealing exclusively with delinquents. Regarding boys this was certainly the case. In 1959, 95% of boys sent to Approved Schools were offenders; only 36% of girls admitted were offenders.

Table 3
Success Rates 1933-1967: Showing Number of Boys and Girls
Who Avoided Reconviction in the Three Years Following
Discharge from an Approved School

Year	%
1933	77
1938	75
1941	71
1944	63
1947	66
1950	63
1953	62
1955	56
1956	50
1959	43
1960	43
1962	38
1963	35
1964	32
1965	36
1966	35
1967	34

Compiled from Home Office figures provided by Gill, 1974

The Children and Young Persons Act 1933 had given the
Courts a range of powers in respect of juvenile offenders.
Amongst these were: absolute or conditional discharge; a fine;
a probation order; a fit person order; an approved school order;
detention, for a limited period, in a remand home; attendance
centre for a specified number of hours; borstal or prison for
young people aged 16 years and over. Until 1948 whipping was
also allowed as a punishment for young people. It was not until
the Criminal Justice Act 1948 that children of 14 years and
over could be placed in Detention Centres, the first of which
opened in 1952.

A 'child', under the 1933 Act, was defined as someone
between the ages of 8 and 14 years, and a 'young person' as
someone between 14 and 18 years of age. Under the Children
Act 1963, Courts were required not to send a child under 10
years of age to an Approved School unless they were satisfied
that he or she could not be dealt with otherwise.

Children could be admitted to an Approved School for the following reasons:

1. Those found guilty of an offence which, in the case of an adult, would be punishable with imprisonment.
2. Children who were found to be in need of care, protection or control. Included under this section were children against whom offences had been committed, including bodily injury and a number of other offences ranging from incest to neglect, procuring and allowing persons under 16 years of age to be in brothels.
3. A child in the care of the Children's Department of the Local Authority, where the Court was satisfied that he or she was refractory and that it was expedient to send the child to an Approved School.
4. A child or young person currently under the supervision of a Probation Officer, and brought back to the Court because of the child's behaviour.
5. A child or young person who was in the care of the Local Authority as a 'fit person' where the Authority thought he or she should be sent to a school and the Court agreed or a child who ran away from the care of a fit person.
6. Those who had been brought before the Court for failure to attend school.

In 1956 the Ingleby Committee was appointed by Parliament to consider, amongst other things, the working of the juvenile courts and the Approved Schools. The Report was presented in 1960 and exposed the conflict between justice and welfare in the Juvenile Court system (Ingleby, 1960). The Court remained a criminal court primarily concerned with the trying of offences, governed by the law of evidence in criminal cases (with a few special provisions). However, the Court was also to have regard to the welfare of the child. It was sometimes difficult for these two principles to be reconciled, for:

> ...*criminal responsibility is focused on an allegation about some particular act isolated from the character and needs of the defendant, whereas welfare depends on a complex of personal, family and social considerations (Ingleby ,1960).*

The Report recognised that if the welfare of the child is the paramount consideration in deciding whether any State intervention should be made, then ideally such intervention should not be limited by the need to wait until one or more factors had been established. It came down, however, in favour of the prevailing system, stating:

> *The strength of the present system is that it is reasonably acceptable to the Community because it satisfies the general demand that there should be some defined basis for State intervention ... Further, experience has shown that the range of circumstances which come within the category of offences...is wide enough to cover virtually all cases where there may be good cause for intervention.*

The dual function of the Court, Ingleby admitted, left scope for apparent injustice. The Court could appear to deal with a case on the grounds of the offence and then deal with it on the basis of the child's needs. For example a child charged with a petty theft, which justice would suggest would result in no great penalty, could lead, after a full investigation into the child's home circumstances, to the Court deciding to remove the child from home for a prolonged period. Conversely a child with good home circumstances, in Court for a fairly serious offence, might be allowed home with a fine.

Ingleby, however, rejected the idea of a non-judicial or of a quasi-judicial tribunal to replace the Juvenile Court maintaining that it was necessary for the proper protection of those who are the subject of proceedings and that only a Court of Law should have the power to interfere with personal liberty. As far as the existing practice of removing a child or young person from home was concerned, 'no such order shall be made unless the Court is satisfied that the need of protection or discipline evidenced before it cannot be met without removal from home' (Ingleby, 1960). This was an important point and opened the way to a further consideration before an Approved School order was made.

Although Ingleby had argued that the existing arrangements were, for the most part, satisfactory continuing concern about the rise in juvenile offending ensured that the debate on the most effective way of dealing with young offenders did not go away. The number of children and young people found guilty of indictable offences in a Magistrate's Court had grown considerably since 1938, the base year used in the Reports of the Work of the Children's Department, published by the Home Office at three year intervals between 1951 and 1969 (Home Office, 1951; 1955; 1961).

In 1938 the total number of persons under 17 years of age found guilty of indictable offences was 28,116, which was 35.8% of the total number of all offenders found guilty. There was concern about the rapid increase in the number of offenders in the early years of World War II. It was during this period that the number of Approved Schools rose from 104 in 1938 to 145 in 1945.

After rising to a peak of 43,583 young offenders in 1941 numbers fell to 35,694 in 1947, rising again in the late 1940s and early 1950s. After 1952, however, the number of offenders suddenly dipped in the years 1953-56. During this period the number of children in Approved Schools fell from 9,416 in 1952-53 to 6,810 in 1955-56, the lowest total since 1935. This led to the closure of 32 schools between 1950 and 1955. The decline in offending ended in 1957 when the numbers rose to 45,107, and continued to rise rapidly, reaching 67,784 by 1963. For the next three years there was again a reduction of recorded offenders, though this was in part due to the implementation of Section 16 of the Children and Young Persons Act 1963, which raised the age of criminal responsibility from 8 to 10 years. The number of offenders began to rise sharply in 1968, reaching 95,900 (see Table 4)

Table 4
Number of Juveniles (Boys and Girls) Found Guilty of Indictable Offences 1938-1968

Year	Number
1938	28116
1941	45583
1947	35694
1950	42415
1953	38690
1955	35513
1960	57360
1963	67784
1965	62870
1968	95900

Compiled from figures presented by the Home Office ,1966 and NACRO, 1985a

The age distribution of young offenders was well illustrated by the figures for 1965. They showed that the number of boys under 14 years of age found guilty of an indictable offence was

22,376 and the number for boys between the ages of 14 and 17 years was 32,818. The older age range was clearly the peak period of offending. The comparative figure for girls was under 14 years, 2,697 and over 14 years , 4,979. These figures show the low rate of offending by girls, although proportionately the numbers show a greater increase in crime by girls than boys as compared with the 1938 figures.

In an attempt to respond to the growth in juvenile crime an experiment had been undertaken in 1949 by the Police in Liverpool, based on their normal practice of cautioning an offender. A number of police officers were formed into a Juvenile Liaison Team, with the task of prevention of juvenile crime.

The Juvenile Liaison Team was concerned mainly with younger children whose offences were trivial and who had not appeared in the Juvenile Court for any other offences. The main objects of the scheme were to secure the cooperation of the family and the school, to bring to the attention of the statutory and voluntary services the factors which may have been leading to the child's offending and to follow up the caution by keeping in touch with the child and his or her family until satisfied that the child was unlikely to offend again. The Home Office considered that the scheme had met with modest success in reducing offending, that it had led to earlier intervention in a child's delinquent behaviour and that it had improved relationships between the public and the police. The scheme was, therefore, commended by the Secretary of State 'as a sound method for dealing with incipient juvenile crime' and was adopted in a number of other areas in England (Home Office, 1955). This method of dealing with very young offenders was to be the basis of a major strategy in the 1980s, and will be explored further in Chapter 11.

Confidence in the value and efficacy of the Approved Schools as a method for dealing with young offenders was high during the early years of the Schools. Gill (1974) quoted Borgat (1941) who had observed:

> *It is better by far to send a boy away to be brought up a good citizen than to leave him indelibly impressed with the mark of a sordid home environment, probably to add to such conditions himself when he reaches manhood. The pity is not that such boys (i.e. Approved School boys) gain an advantage but that this advantage cannot be enjoyed by all.*

The Curtis Report (1946) expressed general satisfaction with the work of the Approved Schools service: 'In the main the Approved Schools seem to us to be well conducted in a humane and experimental spirit'. It commented on the value of the all year round service offered by the schools for children who were often unmanageable in ordinary children's homes. It was not, however, uncritical of the system.

The chief fault we find in the schools for boys are insufficient feminine influence and a tendency in some of them to regimentation ... With regard to Senior Girls Schools, we have some doubts about the value of institutional treatment.

The 'Establishment' showed their general approval of the system by being involved in a number of ways. New schools were opened by senior members of the Government, they were visited on special anniversaries by national figures. The *Approved Schools Gazette* records a number of these visits. In 1957 the Joint Parliamentary Under Secretary of State for the Home Department went to Risley Hall School to open the new gymnasium. The Home Secretary, R.A. Butler, visited Court Lees School in November 1957 for its centenary celebrations and the Archbishop of York visited East Moor School for its centenary. In March 1960, Butler visited Greystokes School and in May 1960 a Parliamentary Under Secretary visited Essex Homes School to open a new classroom block.

As well as these clear gestures of Government recognition of the importance of the system up to and beyond the early 1960s, the Ingleby Report (1960) also came down firmly in favour, with some minor modifications, of the Approved School system.

Acquiring work skills - an essential element in training
(The Royal Philanthropic School in the 1890s)

Digging for victory and training
(Barnardos Druids Heath School, 1941)

Five

Strengths and Weaknesses

After World War II, there had been a major effort to improve and update the child care services and to modernise the law in respect of children in need. The introduction of the Children Act 1948 led to the creation of Children's Departments in each local authority. Some of these Departments began to question the validity of the distinction between a deprived and a delinquent child. One local authority, Oxfordshire, pursued a policy of not recommending any children for placement in Approved Schools and indeed only one child in the County was so placed in 1964. The Children's Officer during this period was Barbara Kahan, who was later to play a major part in the restructuring of the emergent Community Home Schools in her capacity as Deputy Director of the DHSS Social Work Service.

Packman (1981) identified the growing disenchantment with the Approved Schools amongst the new child care officers in the Children's Departments. She observed that the boarding school structures and the stress on discipline, training and education contrasted with the prevailing child care model of substitute homes based on the belief in the value of close personal relationships. Further disadvantages of the schools were that they were located unevenly throughout the country and the children and young people were often placed long distances from home, making it difficult to sustain and improve the child's relationships with his or her parents. Child care officers, who were generally aiming at rehabilitation of the child, saw this as a serious obstacle.

In the Approved School system emphasis had been placed on trying to find the school that would best meet the child's needs. To this end a system of classifying schools had been developed. Prior to 1943 the Courts required the Home Office to name the school to which a child would be sent, but in that year Aycliffe School, near Darlington, became the first Classifying School. After World War II four more Classifying

Schools for boys and two for girls were established.

The 1946 publication *Making Citizens* observed that it was the aim that every child committed to an Approved School should be sent firstly to a Classifying School. The latter were staffed by educational psychologists and teachers competent to assess the abilities, temperament and character of the child who would spend from one to three months in the school. Following these deliberations it would be decided which Approved School would be most suitable for the child. Two factors in particular influenced the choice of school, age and religion.

As the schools were divided into junior, intermediate and senior, children were placed in schools appropriate to their age group. They were also placed according to their religious persuasion. Other factors included the child's vocational orientation, so that as far as possible, especially with older children, a school offering appropriate trade training was chosen. There was also one school for boys with high intelligence, and three short-term schools. Smaller schools were considered appropriate for children with a special need for individual attention.

The Curtis Report (Curtis, 1946) raised some concerns about the concept of classification. Although it was acknowledged that the system was too new for a definitive judgement to be made, concern was expressed that, when a child had spent time in a particular school, to move him or her seemed more like an interruption of rather than a beginning of training, and valuable time could have been lost. This view was shared by the schools at the 'receiving end'. The opinion was that the time in a classifying school merely unsettled the child, who was discouraged from forming relationships in a place of temporary stay. It was believed that the proper place for classification was in the remand home. One Headmaster expressed his scepticism of the system by observing that his school appeared to be classified as a school for enuretics.

The London County Council adopted the practice of adding classification to the duties of its remand homes, Stamford House (boys) and Cumberlow Lodge (girls). Throughout the remainder of England, however, the norm was to be that of having separate remand homes and basing classifying schools on a campus with an adjoining training school, which was one of the options for placement of the child.

One difficulty with the classifying system was that there was often only a very limited number of vacancies in the Schools. As a result a child often had to be placed wherever there was a vacancy in order to avoid the classifying school becoming congested with children awaiting their 'ideal' placement. This was certainly the experience of the writer during his period on the staff of Stamford House in London between 1962-65.

The classifying schools tended to recruit a number of people of high calibre to become part of a multi-disciplinary team of teachers, instructors, care staff, psychologists and psychiatrists. They became increasingly adept at applying their knowledge and skills and set some high standards of practice. They also served to offer good experience to a number of staff who eventually went on to work in the Approved Schools.

An important element in the system was that the Schools were open institutions:

> *...considerable freedom to come and go is found in many of the schools and this, in view of the behaviour of many boys and girls before admission, shows considerable enterprise and courage on the part of those responsible. There is a healthy absence of high walls except in a few old buildings and locked doors are very rare (Curtis, 1946).*

This was not generally realised by the public, or even by some police officers, and led to ill-informed references in the 1970s to 'incarceration'.

In many instances the open regimes were operated with a degree of ambivalence, due to the difficulties and concerns associated with children who ran away from the schools. A study produced in 1971, *Absconding from Approved Schools* (Home Office Research Unit, 1971), confirmed that it was comparatively easy for a boy or girl to abscond. Absconding was regarded as a serious matter and persistent absconders would be transferred to a Special Secure Unit (of which there were three), or returned to Court for an extended Approved School Order or an order for Borstal Training. The research showed that 39% (318 out of 822) of a sample of boys admitted to training schools during 1963 and 57% (371 out of 657) of a sample of girls admitted to training schools during 1963-67 absconded at least once. Six per cent of the boys who absconded and 12.8% of the girls were persistent absconders, i.e. had absconded at least six times during any one continuous period of training.

An 'absconder' was defined as a boy or girl who was absent without leave and who failed to return before midnight on the day of absence. A 'bound breaker' was someone absent without leave but who returned before midnight. Records of absconding and bound breaking were kept from 1956 until 1968. During that period the numbers continued to rise. In 1956 a total of 2,682 incidents of absconding and bound breaking was recorded for boys, and 1,317 for girls. By 1968 the figures had increased to 8,884 for boys and 2,144 for girls. During this period the total annual numbers in the Approved Schools slightly increased (see Table 5).

Table 5
The Numbers Absconding and Bound Breaking from Approved Schools 1956-1968

	Boys	Girls
1956	2682	1317
1957	3000	1200
1958	3900	1250
1959	3800	2050
1961	4750	2300
1960	4700	1700
1962	4550	1256
1963	4600	1200
1964	4900	1500
1965	5100	1700
1966	5450	2200
1967	7060	2100
1968	8884	2144

Compiled from figures given in Home Office Research Unit, 1971

The study of absconding suggested two possible reasons for the increase: firstly a growth in the number of difficult children in Approved Schools (although it was acknowledged there was no specific evidence that this was so), and secondly, and most probably, the greater freedom within the schools and the less severe penalties attached to absconding. These views may be correct but they do beg a number of questions, particularly as to why schools became less restrictive. Possible explanations for this trend were that society had become less authoritarian in the manner in which it managed children and young people and the schools had reflected some of these changes in attitude. The children also had become less likely than earlier generations to accept restrictions which appeared foreign to their earlier experiences.

Previously the response to absconding had been very harsh. The Curtis Committee (Curtis, 1946) reported that, in one girls school, the practice was to cut short the hair of first time absconders. If a girl absconded a second time she was given an Eton crop and if a third time she had her hair shaved and was dressed in a shapeless twill smock. This type of response was not approved of by the Committee and in the 1960s it is unlikely to have been tolerated by the pupils.

Absconding continued to be a serious concern for the schools. As Rose (1967) observed, absconding was seen as a reflection on and rejection of the schools regime and a reminder to the other residents that they were in the schools by compulsion. He suggested that for those who liked being where they were, or were prepared to put up with it, this did not matter but for those who did not like it, it increased their unsettlement. The Home Office Research Unit study (1971) indicated that there were few solitary absconders. When two or more, girls especially, absconded together evidence suggested that this aroused tension in the entire school, followed by a spate of absconding before the school settled down again.

Other negative factors associated with absconding were that offences in the locality of the school led to local hostility, lengthy spells of time spent by staff recovering absconders and concern and anxiety by Police and the children's parents. One of the most serious of the concerns was that children who absconded were likely to re-offend whilst absent and that, in the long term, these children became more likely to continue offending. The study concluded that absconding was a sufficiently serious problem to detract from the benefits of open training.

Despite the very real problem of absconding it should be remembered that the greater majority of children in Approved Schools were not persistent absconders and that many did not abscond at all. Millham et al. (1975) put the question:

How is it then, that such schools, with unwilling clientele, who are often experiencing the inevitable deprivations of residential school life for the first time, do not disintegrate into riot and mass breakouts? What aspects of social control keep these institutions the quiet, often contented places visitors find them to be?

A key objective was the achievement of school regimes that were concerned not merely with the short term goals of control and management of the children but with fundamental change in their values and attitudes. Gittins (1952) had noted these dilemmas:

The great desire of the boy is to get out, to go on licence. To achieve this he seeks to exhibit a socially acceptable pattern of behaviour, yet ... if the essential attitude remains the same, the training is basically ineffective.

This problem remained unresolved when Millham et al. carried out their study 20 years after Gittins' remarks. In the survey of Schools the most common reward was the awarding of points which earned promotion to a higher grade, and also resulted in increased pay and an early release:

Within such a system release itself becomes a utilitarian reward for conforming to certain norms of desired behaviour rather than being a recognition that a boy has reformed either his beliefs or his behaviour.

The sanctions used also tended to reinforce pragmatic value systems. Amongst the sanctions found were forfeiture of pay, reduction of home leave, caning and the threat of transfer.

The problem of reconciling the need for reasonable levels of conformity with the aim of having a lasting impact on the behaviour of the individuals remained a pre-occupation of the Approved School service, if not always of every school. There were two main strands of thinking about the kind of regime that could achieve these joint aims. Gill (1974) described the first as placing emphasis on the overall effect of the school regime, which it was believed would result in pupils benefiting from the socialising function of the school in terms of the transmission of the values, culture and norms of the wider society. The second method, which did not begin to be widely used until the 1960s, was to individualise the approach to the children. Under this system children were encouraged to discuss their individual problems and in some instances to 'act out' their feelings of aggression and insecurity. Especial emphasis was placed on the forming of warm and accepting relationships between the adult and the child. The impact of this philosophy could be seen in practical terms in the move away from the old block system to the house unit system.

In the traditional model emphasis was on order, routine, awarding of merit marks, supervised activities and regular church attendance. Although there were a number of clear similarities between the traditional and the quasi-liberal systems, such as occasional checking of numbers to ensure that all were still present, there were distinct differences. In the latter system greater emphasis was placed on the importance of house groups and time spent in unorganised activities. The counting of children throughout the day was indicative of the tension and mistrust that existed in varying degrees in the schools, whatever the system.

This tension seemed inevitable given the compulsory nature of the children's placements, the previous histories of many of the residents and the fluid intake practices. Children were admitted at almost any time during the year. They could also be discharged at any time during the year although, as the schools had more control over this, discharges tended to be at natural intervals in the school calendar.

Linked with the practice of counting was the almost constant supervision of pupils, in both models. The older model saw the staff primarily in a supervisory role. In the newer model, whilst retaining this role, it was expected that staff would enable the children to form closer trusting relationships with them. In some schools some pupils who had earned a greater degree of trust were allowed out unescorted.

Dunlop (1974) identified the main characteristics of a number of Approved Schools and made an analysis of their long term impact on the children's behaviour. Nine intermediate age range (13-15 years) schools for boys were studied. Their success rates ranged from 54% to 19%. The amount of emphasis that schools placed on certain aspects of training seemed to determine how successful boys would be. The single aspect of training which was appreciated by the largest number of boys was training for work. The closest rival to this was the chance to develop responsibility and maturity. Training based on those aspects held in highest esteem by the boys led to greater success rates by the school. The schools where training for work played an important role were the most successful. Dunlop observed that:

...at these schools the boys tended to believe that they had been given opportunities for growth in maturity and responsibility. Schools which emphasised some other aspects of training - leisure activities, education, religion - were relatively unsuccessful but their failure seemed to stem more from a comparative neglect of trade training in their programmes rather than from their promotion of these unexceptionable alternatives.

The study looked closely at the reasons why trade training schools were more successful and suggested that it was because something was offered which both boys and staff agreed was valuable; that a structure was provided in which delinquent behaviour was discouraged; that clear roles and functions were established; and, finally, that adult-young person relationships were allowed to be formed in a context of real life interaction. The study concluded that schools which concerned themselves with good relationships were no more successful than others. It was also pointed out that a relationship-orientated regime, did not preclude there being a work training emphasis.

Trade training had been a feature of the early years of the Approved Schools, but as was noted in the Sixth Report of the Children's Department (Home Office, 1951) the motivation for this had been somewhat different from what later developed:

In the past the motive for this emphasis was to provide an exercise in discipline and the duller the task the better it thought to fulfil this function, also whatever task was undertaken, there had to be a profit for the institution to help keep down maintenance costs.

Many of these attitudes were no longer in evidence when Dunlop's study was carried out. They do, however, illustrate the importance attitudes can have in changing the same type of activity from a burden to an incentive, from a punishment to an opportunity for self respect and achievement. The Home Office came to recognise the need to ensure that trade training was relevant to the general employment market. Thus it was observed in the Seventh Report (Home Office, 1955) that while farming and gardening still played an important part, the scope of vocational training had been broadened to include a variety of workshop crafts.

Millham et al. (1975) were also impressed by the value and significance of trade training, and observed that trade training was similar in both intermediate and senior boys schools. In the schools which catered for the more able boys there were well equipped engineering workshops and, in most, provision for horticulture, building, carpentry, plumbing and painting and decorating. Many schools had extensions built by the boys, including swimming baths, staff houses and administration blocks.

Millham et al. did, however, record some problems with the trade training system. The first was the way in which each trade in a school operated separately and in competition with other trades 'for resources, for favour, for promising boys, and for time'. The second problem was that there could be times, depending on the occupancy levels, when the departments were under-used. It was suggested that the facilities could be shared with main stream education. In a few instances this did happen, for example at Wellesley School in Northumberland whose facilities were used by local schools.

Until 1961 the Home Office published in its reports, statistics recording the number of boys and girls from Approved Schools who had obtained employment. Clearly much effort was taken in ensuring the young people obtained employment on release from the schools and there was considerable pride and satisfaction at what was achieved. Of 2,936 boys of employable age released in 1959 only 161 were reported as not being placed in employment. A whole range of occupations, together with the numbers engaged, was listed, including the building trade, carpentry, engineering, railway work, factory work. For girls the results were equally impressive. Of 806 girls of working age released, only 66 were recorded as unemployed. Most went into shop work, others into clerical employment or into domestic service.

These achievements were all the more remarkable in view of the general level of intellectual ability of most of the children who were placed in Approved Schools. The only measure available for this was intelligence quotient tests which were standard practice at that time. Subsequently many have doubted the reliability of such methods. According to Rose (1967) most boys had intelligence quotients of below 100 (see Table 6).

Table 6
The Intelligent Quotient of Boys in Approved Schools 1967

IQ	%
<70	5
70-80	10
80-100	70
>100	15

Compiled from data in Rose, 1967

Although the majority of boys in the schools had IQs slightly lower than the national average, they were certainly not low enough to be considered educationally subnormal or seriously ineducable. The work results of the children were certainly not as low as their previously poor attainments would have led one to expect (Millham et al., 1975).

This research also had shown only limited evidence of disruptive and anti-staff behaviour in mainstream schools by Approved School boys prior to admission. The prevailing problems exhibited had been of backwardness, inclination to truancy, isolation from other children and withdrawn attitudes to staff.

Formal education in Approved Schools was generally considered to be quite good, especially since most of the pupils had done their best to avoid school or at least teachers. Curtis (1946) reported that, in general, the standard of education did not fall below the norm, and in at least one respect, was better, i.e. the size of classes in Approved Schools was much smaller. A recurrent criticism of formal education in the Schools was that teaching methods tended to be antiquated because teachers were said to be out of touch with the mainstream of education, although they did have the opportunity for refresher courses on teaching techniques (Rose, 1967).

Most of the boys coming into the Schools had poor school attainments and, for these boys, there was much to commend the Approved School educational system. There were small groups available for teaching for almost any length of time, facilities that were certainly not ungenerous when compared with day school provision and often no examination requirements or syllabus demands to limit what could be done.

Few schools, however, capitalised on the advantages offered by the fewer numbers and flexible structures (Millham et al., 1975). A number of examples were given to illustrate this point. In one school only 47% of pupils improved in their reading, 20% did so in arithmetic and 5% in spelling. In another school, where greater emphasis was placed on trade training, this was clearly reflected in the classroom attainment of the boys. In a therapeutic community, the pupils did increase their arithmetic attainments but not their reading: indeed in this school the pupils were often so preoccupied with their therapeutic drama of confrontation that the classrooms remained locked and the trade training departments virtually fossilised.

The study came to two main conclusions about formal education, based on a survey of 18 Approved Schools undertaken in the closing years of the system , 1969-1972.

The first was that many of the schools operated on the negative principle of that which is best is whatever keeps the boys occupied, thereby missing the chance to explore the wide range of opportunities available.

The second and positive conclusion was that the most successful schools educationally and culturally were those which expected a high standard from the pupils. In these schools involved staff led small groups in a sustained way through a range of activities, including evening activities and summer camps. This consistent educational approach was linked with the workshops and these in particular represented 'integrated studies at their best' (Millham et al., 1975).

Although there were no examination requirements for the schools as a body there were opportunities for individual boys and girls to be entered for public examinations. The Approved Schools release system did present some obstacles to this, as was observed in the 1966 Report of the Children's Department (Home Office, 1966). The introduction of the Certificate of Secondary Education examinations had presented difficulties since there was only one examination a year whereas three opportunities would be needed if pupils were to be able to take the examinations, without having their release date delayed.

There is very little evidence of the Home Office and the Department of Education working together in respect of the Approved Schools. The Children's Department Report of 1967-1969 stated that HM Inspector of Schools had shown a helpful interest over many years and had worked closely with Children's Department Inspectors (Home Office, 1969). There were no examples given as to the nature of this helpful interest.

Outdoor activities were a prominent feature of most

Approved Schools curricula. Sporting facilities, including swimming pools and gymnasiums and sports fields were available in most schools. Entry into local as well as inter-school events was the norm as it was considered that this encouraged pride in one's school and a healthy competitiveness. Participation in the Duke of Edinburgh's Award Scheme stimulated many to organise 'adventure' type activities. The Eighth Children's Department Report (Home Office, 1961) observed that, in the four years in which schools had taken part in the scheme, 95 Silver Awards and 82 Bronze Awards had been gained. The Wellesley Nautical School was visited in June 1960 by HRH The Duke of Edinburgh, who presented seven Silver Awards to the boys. Schools also entered courses arranged by the Outward Bound Trust. Many arranged summer camps, partly to give the children a holiday.

Home leave was restricted to 24 days a year. The Ingleby Report (1960) had urged that more discretion be permitted in the amount of home leave allowed. Until this time the prevailing attitude was that contact with home and parents should be of a very limited nature. This policy had sprung from the belief that parental contact often undid the work of the schools. This thinking was certainly not as prevalent in 1960 as it had been a decade earlier but the leave system did sustain it. Ingleby (1960) attempted to redress the balance and commented that 'home leave properly used, can be of great therapeutic value ... for younger children especially'.

Shortly after the Ingleby Report the Eighth Report from the Children's Department (Home Office, 1961) also acknowledged the advantages of greater parental contact. There was a growing belief among social workers that their task was to support parents in the exercise of their responsibilities, not to supplement them. It was argued that, despite the hazards in pursuing such a policy, it was necessary as 'it is difficult to find an adequate substitute for the security and affection that even a poor and ill-managed home can provide'. This major change in emphasis on the role and status of parents had been rapidly developing since the Children Act 1948 .

Parents were required to pay contributions for the maintenance of their children in Approved Schools. The amount paid could either be determined by the Court, taking into account the parents means, or by agreement with the local authority which collected the fees. The policy reflected the continuing belief that parents should take some responsibility for their child's behaviour and delinquency. The actual amounts collected were an insignificant part of the total cost of keeping a child in an Approved School. The average weekly contributions paid by parents in the years 1964-65 brought in a total of £161,936 in a total expenditure of £7,532,092. The amount of effort involved and the resentment generated in the collection of such a relatively small sum made the value of the practice questionable.

In the early 1960s the average length of stay in an Approved School was 20 months. The length a child could be detained was determined by his or her age on committal. A child under the age of 12 years and 4 months at the date of committal could be kept until he or she reached the age of 15 years and 4 months. If a child had reached the age of 12 years and 4 months at the date of committal, the child could be kept until the expiry of 3 years from that date or until reaching the age of 19 years, whichever was the shorter period.

Table 7

Length of Stay of Boys and Girls in Approved Schools 1966

Stay	Senior		Intermediate		Junior	
	Boys	Girls	Boys	Girls	Boys	Girls
18 Months	125	116	85	94	64	85
2 Years	70	73	92	94	69	79
3 Years	54	58	70	59	96	78
4 Years	0	0	0	0	68	57

Compiled from Rose, 1967

Table 7 indicates that, in practice, children admitted to schools in the senior age range were likely to remain for the shortest time and that children in the junior age range tended to stay in Schools much longer. A few boys (1%) remained up to five years. The average stay for children in all categories of Approved School was under two years.

The Managers of the Approved School had the power and the responsibility to determine, usually on the recommendation of the Head of School, when a child should be released on licence. Under the Rules for Approved Schools, managers were empowered to place a child on licence as soon as he or she had made sufficient progress in training. With this object in view all the child's personal circumstances, including the family situation, had to be reviewed towards the end of the first year of placement and after that as often as necessary but at least quarterly. In practice, it was recommended that reviews began in the first year.

The managers and the head of the school had therefore considerable discretion in regard to a child's discharge date. During times of pressure on the schools, particularly when there was a heavy demand for places, children tended to be released after shorter periods than at other times. This point was made in the Sixth Report of the Children's Department. 'In war time, it became necessary to reduce the period of training in order to deal with the rapid increase in the number of committals' (Home Office, 1951). There were also occasions when boys who were good at sports or a craft were kept in the school for a longer period than less able children.

In two of the three major crises in Approved Schools history, discharge practices were a significant factor. These incidents will be considered in more detail in Chapter 6 but at this point it is of interest to note, for example, that in the Standon Farm School enquiry it was found that the managers had left the decision about licensing to the Headmaster. In the Carlton School Disturbances it was found that the Headmaster, in an effort to arrest the declining success rate, had recommended to the managers that no boy should be released unless he had a strong chance of success. As a result of this policy the average length of stay at the school increased from 18 to 23 months. The success rate of the school rose from 63.3% to 70.9% over the seven years the policy was in operation but it culminated in major disturbances.

All the children 'released' (this was the official term) before the maximum period of their possible detention were released on licence. This period on licence lasted until the expiry of the maximum period of detention or until the young person reached the age of 21 years. During the time on licence the young person could be recalled by the managers to complete the period of detention. In practice the number recalled was never more than 352 in any one year.

The young person was also subject to a period of two years supervision and after care. The After Care Officers were located in a variety of agencies. Originally the system for boys operated in the main urban areas and was based in schools in and around these areas. The Officers, the majority of whom were untrained, had large case loads which required much travelling. Of necessity they tended to concentrate on crisis activity.

The Probation Service became involved in after care work, originally on a voluntary basis and after 1952 on a statutory basis, by arrangement with the school managers. There was, however, some division of opinion about the wisdom of asking probation offices to undertake this task because of their close association with the courts. Children's Departments were also widely used, especially for girls. Increasingly the pressure on staff in the schools did not allow them to do their own after care work. Where they did there were obvious benefits of having a person with whom the boy or girl had formed a helping relationship.

By 1965 only 15% of boys were supervised by Approved School Welfare Officers. The majority were supervised by Probation Officers and a large number by Children's Departments (see Table 8 below). The after care service had very limited resources and as a result the provision offered was of a rather basic nature.

Table 8
Aftercare Supervision

Supervisor	Boys	Girls
Welfare Officer	15%	0%
Probation Officer	43%	65%
Child Care Officer	38%	25%
School Staff	3%	8%

Ingleby (1960) recommended that there should be greater recognition of the importance of this aspect of the Approved School service and that thought be given to ways of ensuring a more effective after care system. It was proposed that the Probation Service and the local authority should be the after care agents but responsibility should rest with the individual school. Despite these exhortations after care was a good idea that was never really implemented to any great degree because of the manpower and cost implications.

The Approved School system was clearly very complex and relied largely on a sound but flexible structure operated by senior staff with enough insight, integrity, and general strength of character to manage the multi-disciplinary staff team, the disturbed and delinquent young people, and the fabric and grounds and finances of a school. Occasionally when these qualities were absent major difficulties ensued, with not only the school concerned but the whole Approved School system becoming suspect.

Six

Pressures for Change

There were three notorious major incidents which led to public concern about the efficacy of the Approved Schools and the quality of their staff. The first of these incidents occurred in 1947 when, in the words of the Sixth Report of The Children's Department (Home Office, 1951), 'there occurred the gravest crime in the history of the Approved Schools'. The incident, at Standon Farm School in Staffordshire, began when nine boys who had decided to abscond stole rifles from the school's army cadet force armoury. They shot dead one of the school's staff who had come across them. Apparently their intention had been to murder the headmaster and then steal a car in which to abscond. The boys were quickly caught and all were subsequently sentenced to varying lengths of further detention. There was widespread public concern and a committee of enquiry was set up to investigate. The Committee found that the crime was the result of the grievances of the ringleaders. These grievances, which had built up over a period of time, were centred around the deferment of release; the isolated position of the School; the lack of recreational activities; the severity of the discipline, which led to the loss of the few privileges the boys enjoyed: and the use of collective punishments. This type of regime, it was concluded, led, in a school of 65 boys, to an overwhelming hostility to the headmaster. It transpired that the headmaster had exclusive control of the licensing of the boys. One of the main recommendations of the enquiry was that the school managers should play an active part in reviewing the circumstances of each boy at the end of his first year at an Approved School and frequently thereafter. Better communication with boys and parents about licensing procedure was also recommended. The headmaster of the school was subsequently dismissed and the school closed.

The Standon Farm incident made it clear that there was a need for a proper balance between the considerable powers of the Headmaster and the Board of Managers in Approved Schools.

The incidents also exposed the considerable vulnerability of the system to public analysis and criticism. On this particular occasion the system managed to stand up well to this. This is well illustrated by Lane (1968) who records in his study, *The Public Image of the Approved School System*, the observations of the Manchester Guardian for 27 June 1947, which, he suggested, summed up the press response to the Standon Farm events:

> *The report (of the enquiry) is far from condemning of the whole system of institutional treatment of young delinquents. It is in fact only by comparison with the system's success elsewhere that the failures of Standon Farm stand condemned.*

In later years, however, this general reaction to the incident seems to have been forgotten. It was instead recalled along with other incidents to question the validity of the Approved School system. Interestingly *The Manchester Guardian* was to play a major part in this change of attitude.

The next major incident occurred in August 1959 and became known as the 'Disturbance at Carlton School'.

Although no one was killed in these events they attracted much attention because the press were on the spot to record much of what happened and, as a result, this led to more concern than in the Standon Farm incident. In the Carlton School happenings, groups of boys openly rebelled against the authority of the school's staff. They took part in a mass absconsion, brought in the press and generally aired a number of grievances against the headmaster and his staff. These included allegations of ill treatment of the boys by the staff, of lengthy detention at the school before licensing, of withholding of mail and of failure to send mail out promptly.

A subsequent one man enquiry conducted by Victor Durand QC was ordered by the Home Office. Durand found that some staff had used illicit corporal punishments on boys on regular occasions. It was also established that the headmaster had introduced lengthier than normal periods of detention in the belief that this was necessary to improve the success rate of the school. The managers had allowed the headmaster to make all the decisions about the appropriate time at which boys would be released on licence. The allegations with regard to the mail were found to have some substance but this was put down to mis-management rather than a deliberate policy of withholding or delaying the sending out of mail. The Report found that some of the difficulties had been caused by the abnormally high number of boys at Carlton who presented severe behaviour problems.

It is noteworthy that the licensing problem was almost identical to the Standon Farm practice. Durand said there had been serious mismanagement and bad practice in the school, and apportioned blame for these shortcomings. The mismanagement of the particular incidents were attributed largely to the inadequacies of the deputy headmaster and some infringements of regulations by members of staff. Surprisingly the headmaster emerged from the enquiry relatively well, partly because he was absent at the time of the disturbances and also because of what was said to be other mitigating factors. Durand concluded by making recommendations for improving practice and management. Some of these were specific to Carlton, others were applicable to the Approved Schools in general. The most significant of these was that consideration should be given to providing 'closed facilities' in a number of schools. This suggestion was subsequently taken up and secure units were opened in three of the four Classifying Schools.

The Report also proposed that the salaries of housemasters needed to be reviewed in order to attract a better quality of applicant. It was observed that because of the growing demand for Approved Schools places, Carlton had had to increase its occupancy from 86 to 96 boyd. Durand suggested that there should be more places made available in the Approved School system. He recommended the use of secure rooms for short periods for very difficult and intractable boys.

While accepting that some individuals had been at fault, Durand also made it clear that he believed that the problems had been caused in part by shortcomings in the whole Approved School system. This event had, therefore, been used by the Home Office to strengthen the system by increasing Approved School places, adding secure units and secure rooms and improving the salaries of housemasters.

The popular press had acted with a disregard for the value of the Approved School system. They arrived at the disturbances largely in pursuit of sensational stories and indeed some may have helped prolong the incidents for these reasons. Durand found, that there had been examples of 'regrettable behaviour' by the press. The Carlton School disturbances once again illustrated how vulnerable the Approved Schools were to adverse publicity and also how easily a situation could get out of hand if not carefully managed and controlled.

The last of the serious incidents to have afflicted an Approved School was the Court Lees Affair. This event was of a different order to the previous two occurrences. It did not arise from mass rebellion by the boys but instead from unease felt by a member of staff about the severity of discipline in the school in which he was employed.The affair again involved the press. This time it began with an anonymous letter to *The Guardian* newspaper from an Approved School teacher in March 1967. The writer was very critical of the state of affairs in his place of employment and claimed of regularly hearing boys screaming as they were punished and of near revolt by staff and pupils in the school. This letter and the subsequent developments occurred at a time when the Government of the day had been conducting a public debate on the whole future of the Approved School service.In this climate it was hardly surprising that the press and the public should seize upon this shocking set of allegations to fuel the debate about the future of the Schools.

Matters in the Court Lees affair were brought to a head when the writer of the letter to *The Guardian* sent photographs of the badly bruised bottoms of boys from his school, to the *Daily Mail* who published the pictures. The Home Office made enquiries and identified Court Lees as the school concerned and Ivor Cook as the writer of the correspondence. An official enquiry was then carried out in June 1967 and on the publication of its findings the then Home Secretary, Roy Jenkins, announced the closure of the school with a recommendation that all Approved Schools should phase out the practice of caning as soon as possible. The enquiry also found that the Headmaster had used the cane freely, sometimes as a first response to misbehaviour, that he had used an unauthorised thickness of cane and that he had caned boys who had been made to remove their trousers, all contrary to the Approved School Rules. It was also found that excessive severity had been used on four occasions and that on many other occasions punishments had not been recorded in the punishment book.

The Court Lees Affair and the action of the Home Secretary in closing the School, dismissing the Headmaster and the Deputy Headmaster and ordering that all 115 of the boys either be released early or sent to other schools led to a lengthy and heated debate both in the media and in the Approved School service. Lane (1968) gives a detailed account of the exhaustive press coverage of these events. He notes that in *The Guardian* alone there were 'one hundred articles, news items, leading articles and letters during the fourteen months following the initial article on the subject.'

The Court Lees Affair brought to a head the changing attitudes in the 1960s towards such issues as punishment, trust in the Establishment, the correct and humane response to delinquency and the credibility of people in positions of authority. The media took full advantage of this new found freedom especially when it would be seen to be championing the underdog against a harsh system. These developments, which affected many other contemporary affairs, put the whole Approved School system under considerable pressure. Many of the staff felt betrayed by the Home Secretary's public castigation the main figures involved. There had been an expectation that, as had been the case in the Standon Farm incident and the Carlton School disturbances, there would be some individual disapproval but a general support for the system.

Frank Ebert, an Approved School headmaster and member of the executive council of the Association of Headmasters, Headmistresses and Matrons in Approved Schools, summed up the clear feelings of outrage and betrayal felt by the Approved Schools staff over the affair in the *Approved School Gazette* of March 1968:

> *Mr Jenkins' actions following the Inquiry have done more harm to the Approved Schools than the pseudonymous letters which caused it. Never has morale been so low...Those who as practitioners have direct responsibility for controlling difficult behaviour and creating a school spirit within a caring, helping atmosphere, felt let down by those who, as one eminent head put it, know a lot about Approved Schools without really knowing Approved Schools. When the chips were down we felt cheated. Action was taken without due consultation. Our difficulties were not fully appreciated; our methods of control unsupported.*

Lines of communication between the Approved Schools and the Home Office had broken down at a vital time of crisis.

The Court Lees affair highlighted the major role Government played in the Approved School system and showed how in such a crisis the Government were quickly drawn in and forced to make a public stance. It was the Home Secretary who had to make the decision about what action to take following the publication of the Durand Inquiry report. The matter was the subject of a vote of censure on the Government in the House of Commons in March 1967. This was defeated by 278 votes to 225. It was the subject of a debate in the House of Lords.

This nearness of the Approved School system to Government had been in the past a major factor in the 'special' status of the system. It was to become something which Government wished to see changed so that decisions and responsibility could be located at a much lower level. This will be explored further when consideration is given to the Children and Young Persons Act, 1969.

The Approved School system had emerged from the Industrial and Reform Schools. These institutions had been founded, often with resistance and hostility from those in positions of power who saw them as a soft option, to provide a resource for the many delinquent and near delinquent children and young people wandering the streets of the cities. Public conscience decreed, once it had been awakened, that young people should not just be ignored nor simply treated like adult offenders and sent to prison. It was accepted that as well as punishment children should be taught to become useful citizens and that this reformation could best be carried out in an institution that controlled, trained, educated and cared for young people.

The Children's Act 1933 gave this system renewed status and recognition from the State and the confidence of society in general. It brought together the two forms of school into one, the Approved School, and gave the Courts and the Schools a clear role in the care and management of deprived and delinquent children. Growing child delinquency in a period of great social upheaval during and just after World War II confirmed the vital role the Schools had been given in the general response to juvenile offending.

The Children Act 1948, which brought more cohesion to the

services for children and families in need, also brought into being what was to become a new and influential professional view on the best ways of responding to children in trouble. The well organised small group of senior practitioners who had been held in high regard by an elite group in the Home Office found that the Home Office view began to be broadened as the local authority Children's Officers sought to offer and argue for a wider view of good child care practice. There is little evidence that anything was done to bring together those serving in the Approved School system, with their often long association with the care and management of difficult children, and those working in the Children's Departments with their new, more individually orientated philosophies.

In fact the reverse appears to have been the case with both groups viewing each other with suspicion and in some instances positive hostility. As has been noted earlier, one local authority positively opposed the idea of any of the children going to Approved Schools.

The 1948 Act had given formal recognition of the importance to the child of its natural parents, except in extreme cases. 'The Act was revolutionary in laying on the local authorities a duty to restore those received into care to their own natural home' (Heywood, 1965). Removing a young person from home and training him or her for an honest and productive future, taking only limited account of the child's home and family, was increasingly considered to fall far short of what was required. This thinking continued to develop and by the beginning of the 1960s there was a strong belief in the value of intensive work with the child's family. These views were to be embodied in the Government's White Papers dealing with disturbed and delinquent children. *The Child the Family and Young Offender* (Home Office, 1965) and *Children in Trouble* (Home Office, 1968).

The Approved School service employed a wide range of staff, especially teachers and also many housemasters and housemistresses, who, over the years, had acquired a considerable depth of knowledge and experience in the area of youthful delinquency and general anti-social behaviour. For the most part, they tended to be conservative in their practice. Although as the 1960s progressed there was an increased acknowledgement of the significance of individuality in the young people and greater use of the psychiatric services, most regimes still placed their highest trust in the value of a structured and ordered system offering good training opportunities to achieve the curing of delinquency. Many of the values, however, that the schools continued to inculcate into the young people were no longer held so firmly by society at large. Smartness, self discipline and consideration for others, for example, were not thought so important by many in the freer 'do as you feel' atmosphere of the 'swinging sixties'.

The declining success rates were due in part to the continuing emphasis in the Schools on the values which the children and young people found, on their return to society at large, were no longer prevalent.

Thus conformity to a standard pattern of behaviour was becoming much less praiseworthy and there was in general a greater tolerance of deviation from 'normal' behaviour. Falling success rates were, however, seen by those who questioned the need for children and young people to be removed from home, as evidence of the ineffectiveness, as well as the inappropriateness, of the Approved Schools system. To add to this concern were the growing costs of maintaining Approved Schools. Critics of the system believed that the money spent on sending children to the Schools could be better spent on preventative and other child care services. There was little concern, however, in the 1960s, as there was to be later, about the drain on the public purse and the need to reduce both central and local government spending. During that period the money seemed to flow relatively easily, as the increased expenditure on buildings and staff salaries testify.

The dependence on harsh discipline by the Schools as supposedly typified by the Court Lees affair, the greater attention of the children's departments to families and their worth, the prevailing atmosphere of a growing freedom from constraints, the falling success rates and the escalating costs all contributed to emerging doubts about the Approved School system in Government.

These doubts were also shared by some in the Approved Schools. Their thoughts, however, were that the system needed improving and modernising, not dismantling, for the system had its strength. Its long well established functions were not generally questioned. There were some good buildings, many improved only in recent times, and some excellent resources for skills training and the pursuit of outdoor activities. There were many fine and able people employed in the service. A large number of boys and girls had benefited from the Approved School experience. It had been the best alternative available for many persistent offenders. There had been in fact few options for such young people since, at the time, there was little thought of community based alternatives other than the attendance centres.

The Magistrates, as a body were still very much in favour of the Approved School system and made use of their powers to make Approved School Orders. In 1967 some 5,164 children were admitted to Approved Schools, and a similar number in the following two years.Total occupancy of the Schools had dropped somewhat from 8,213 in 1967 to 7,174 in 1969, but occupancy had remained constant at between 6,500 and 8,000 since 1955. The admission and occupancy figures in the late 1960s were above the average for the 14 year period from 1955-1969.

At the end of the 1960s the Approved Schools remained a significant, even if criticised and questioned, part of the system for dealing with emotionally disturbed and delinquent children. On 31 December 1969 there were 124 Approved Schools in England and Wales, 90 for boys and 34 for girls.How and why this service and system was changed into a system of Community Homes is the subject of the next chapter.

Seven

Seeking New Structures

The 1960s was a decade of great social and legislative innovation. The Report of The Committee on Local Authority and Allied Personal Social Services (Seebohm, 1968), later known as the Seebohm Report, recorded that changes were brought about by additional powers conferred on local authorities by the Mental Health Act, 1959 and The Children and Young Persons Act, 1963; that there were new developments following the Youth Service Albermarle Committee Report on the Youth Service (Albermarle, 1958) the Younghusband Working Party on social workers in health and welfare services (Younghusband, 1959), the Newson Report (1963) and the Plowden Report (1966) on the education services. All of these changes resulted in a general upheaval in local government and especially in the education and social welfare services.

For many in the Approved School service the prospects for the decade did not, in 1960, give much cause for optimism. There was general anxiety about the continuing rise in juvenile delinquency, despite the benefits of a welfare state that had done much to reduce poverty. There was concern also about the manner in which, in 1959, the public confidence in the service had been further undermined by the troublesome events at Carlton School (see Chapter 6).

These concerns were well expressed by Frank Ebert, the Secretary of the Approved Schools Staffs Association (Ebert, 1960). He noted the discernible progress in the field of education in general, with the increase of teacher training to three year courses and the expansion of university and technical educational resources. He observed, however, that no such general optimism pervaded the Approved School service. The mood was rather one of doubt and expectancy. The gloom was to be lifted, in the event, by the findings of the Ingleby Report (1960). This committee had been appointed in 1956 (but did not report until October 1960) to enquire into the working of the law in England and Wales in respect of children and young people, with particular reference to delinquency and children in moral or physical danger. The committee also considered the powers of the local authorities and their adequacy for preventing the neglect of children.

The Ingleby Report emerged as a fairly conservative document, concentrating for the most part on tidying up legislation and procedures. It favoured the retention of the juvenile courts and wished to marginally increase powers of magistrates by, for example, allowing them in some instances to name the actual Approved School to which a youngster would be sent. It also urged the retention of the Approved School system as a separate system, not merged with any other residential provision. The most radical proposal was that the age of criminal responsibility be raised from 10 to 12 years of age (with a possibility of it becoming thirteen or fourteen at some later date). The Report commented on the need for secure provision, as also had the Carlton School Report (1960). The Ingleby Report recommended that closed facilities should be provided for children already in the Approved School system and that 'closed blocks' should be a facility within classifying schools.

Raising of the age of criminal responsibility, the provision of secure accommodation and improved arrangements for after-care were the only recommendations of major significance for the Approved School service. The Ingleby Report was an affirmation of the establishment view of the continuing importance of the Approved Schools as a resource for dealing with juvenile delinquency.

There were some feelings of unease amongst those in the schools regarding the proposal to raise the age of criminal responsibility. If implemented this would result in the removal of the younger age range (8-11 years old) from those then eligible for junior Approved Schools, and more significantly, signalled a discernible shift in attitude towards delinquency and the younger child. Greater emphasis would be placed on the child's need for care and control and less on his criminality.

The Children and Young Persons Act, 1963 took up many recommendations of the Ingleby reports. The Act's main emphasis was on the need for local authorities to promote the welfare of children. To facilitate this, the Act gave the local authorities statutory powers to carry out preventative work with children and families, including the prevention of appearances before juvenile courts. Heywood (1965) observed, that the Act:

...marked a new attitude, a final moving away from the paternalistic protective child centred attitude to positive and skilled family centred work. Case work treatment in the home in itself became a justifiable service and the removal of children from home a form of differentiated treatment for a child, to be used only when he required the particular kind of care and help which the children's department could give him by placing him elsewhere.

Two specific results of the 1963 Act were that the age of criminal responsibility was raised from 8 to 10 years - a cautious response to the Ingleby proposals - and the other was that local authorities were encouraged to designate some remand homes as classifying centres. The Home Office took up the spirit of the 1963 Act in respect of the younger delinquent by asking Police to consult local children's authorities before any action was taken in the juvenile court against children aged between 10 and 12 years. This process was, as will be noted, to be much extended in later years.

There remained, despite the changes brought under the 1963 Act, a growing body of opinion that held that the existing juvenile court system was inappropriate. There were specific indications of the growing support for this view from the recommendations of a Committee, under the Chairmanship of Lord Kilbrandon, appointed by Parliament to review the operation of the law in respect of juveniles in Scotland. The findings of this Committee were published in 1964 (Kilbrandon, 1964) and were later to be enshrined in the Social Work (Scotland) Act, 1968. The major change brought about by this Act was the removal of children under 16 years of age from the jurisdiction of the criminal courts. The Kilbrandon Committee concluded that children appearing before the Courts, whether they had committed an offence or were in need of care and protection, had similar needs both for social and personal care. It was decided that juvenile courts were not the best way of dealing with these problems because of the difficulty of distinguishing, in such a setting, between the needs of justice and the welfare of the child.

Hearings were appointed to deal with all matters formerly dealt with by the juvenile courts. The establishment of the facts, where disputed, remained with the Courts but, except in serious matters such as homicide, the treatment was to be determined by the Children's Hearing Panel.

In 1964 the Conservatives Party was replaced by the Labour Party as the new Government, a change which resulted in a more radical approach to social issues. This was reflected in the field of delinquency, in the White Paper, *The Child, The Family and The Young Offender* (Home Office, 1965). This paper was based on the emerging climate of opinion following the publication of the Ingleby (!960), Kilbrandon (1964), and Longford (1964) reports on juvenile delinquency.

There was general agreement by the three Committees about the nature of the problems that needed to be addressed. The differences came not in the solutions they suggested but rather in the priority which each gave to them. Ingleby suggested 'The long term solution may be in the re-organisation of the various services concerned with the family into a unified family service'. Longford argued that change was needed 'now' as the first step is the establishment of a new family service. Kilbrandon had similar thoughts: 'The existing statutory social services concerned with children's problems should be reorganised into a new comprehensive local department - the social education department' . All stressed the parental role and the assistance needed to aid them in carrying this out. All pointed to the need for the integration of existing services and all emphasised prevention. Ingleby argued for the improvement of the existing structures to achieve these ends, Longford and Kilbrandon urged more radical measures.

In the Government's White Paper, *The Child, The Family and The Young Offender* (Home Office, 1965), the movement towards the creation of an integrated family service was acknowledged as a major overall strategy. Such a service, it was claimed, would more effectively support the family, which in turn would greatly reduce the possibility of the creation of the type of environment in which children became delinquent.

The Government, believed that urgent action was required to reform the existing law in respect of children and young people. Its most radical proposals were that children under 16 years of age should be removed so far as possible from the jurisdiction of the Courts, and that each local authority, through the Children's Committee, be empowered to appoint local family councils to deal with each case in consultation and agreement with parents. Where agreement on the manner of dealing with the child could not be reached with the parents, or where the facts were in dispute, cases would be referred to family courts.

The family court would be a special magistrates court. This court would deal with unresolved issues concerning children under the age of 16 years, with adoption, consent to marry and affiliation orders. The family courts would have the power 'to make any order which is now appropriate to a juvenile court, except that, where long term residential training was considered to be appropriate, the child or young person would be committed to the care of the local authority'.

A further court was proposed for dealing with offenders in the 16 to 21 years of age range. This would be known as the Young Offenders Court, would deal with all but the most serious offences (murder, rape or robbery) and be chaired by a legally qualified person when dealing with indictable offences. The Young Offenders Court would have the same powers then available for dealing with the 17-21 year olds in respect of non-custodial sentences, for example, fines, attendance centres. Prison and Borstal sentences would be replaced by Youth Training Centres (an amalgam of Borstal and Senior Approved Schools) and Young Offenders Institutions. Offenders could be sent to the former for up to two years and to the latter for periods longer than two years.

The major impact of these proposals for the Approved School service would be that provision for the under 16 year olds would be assimilated into a range of residential services available for children at the disposal of the local authority. For those aged 16 years and over such provision would be part of a more general resource for the older offender at the disposal of the Court and still overseen directly by the Home Office.

These proposals were not particularly well received by the Approved School service, as was evident from the editorial of the September 1965 issue of *The Approved School Gazette*. Amongst the questions it suggested the Report had failed to address was the question of manpower; where were 'the additional army of skilled workers necessary to implement these new reforms to come from? 'The editorial questioned the future structures, doubting if the junior and intermediate Schools would relish the thought of being reclassified as children's homes, and asked about the future viability of the voluntary managed schools. Finally, it stated that:

In the present climate of moral breakdown in our society it may be argued that it is hardly the right time to remove from the minds of irresponsible young people the awesome disciplinary influence of appearing in a Court of Law.

Other professionals were more sympathetic to the White Paper proposals. Elizabeth Marshall, the President of the Association of Child Care Officers, declared:

...the incorporation of the Approved Schools within the residential provision of the local authorities children's departments is regarded as an important and necessary development.

The proposals were also welcomed by the Residential Child Care Association and by the Association of Child Care Officers.

The general prospect of the child care service managing the Approved School service clearly appealed to those in the local authority sector while it was less welcome to staff in the Schools. No one was stating that the Approved School service, albeit in a new structure, was unnecessary. Indeed Alice Bacon, the Minister of State for the Home Office said in a speech about the White Paper that 'A good standard of residential care is the whole basis of effective advances in the service as a whole' (Bacon, 1965). This was an unusual public acknowledgement of the significance of residential child care.

The critics of the proposals focused on the folly of abandoning the justice model, with its formal Courts of Law and its residential provision designed primarily for young delinquents. Those who supported the proposals pointed to the benefits the flexibility would bring to the child care service. Bacon (1965) acknowledged that:

...there will always be some very difficult children for whom we have to cater, perhaps in special establishments of the type of the present Approved Schools, but what I have always thought was wrong...is the Approved School order which has always been so inflexible...and so the White Paper envisages the abolition of the Approved School Order, as such, in favour of the committal of care to the local authority...(who) can treat the child in the way best for the child at any particular time.

The 1965 White Paper was intended to provoke informed discussion before final proposals were drawn up and laid before Parliament, and enabled interested parties to think beyond their initial response and offer a formal submission. This the combined Approved School Associations did in a monograph in September 1966. This document indicated a shift in attitude from the initial scepticism and general hostility to the proposals to cautious acceptance of the need for some radical change:

> We have regretted for many years the isolation of Approved Schools from the mainstream of education and indeed, from many activities in the field of child care. We have, therefore, no desire to preserve the status quo (Association of Managers and the Associations of Headmasters, Headmistresses and Matrons and the National Association of Approved Schools, 1966)

The Association stated that although in their view the committing of an offence could not, and should not, avoid the stigma of criminality, the treatment of offenders should never carry this stigma. They proposed that 17 years, not 16, should be the upper age limit for the treatment of offenders. They rejected the idea of the replacement of the juvenile court but proposed that once that court had ruled on a case reference could be made, if necessary, to a 'Family Service' for decisions on treatment.

This was an acknowledgement that the needs of the delinquent and non-delinquent from a troubled family could be similar and of the fact that the whole family, not just the child, needed a response to its problems and difficulties. Approved Schools should, they proposed, be a part of the 'Family Services' resources. They would become boarding schools retaining 'as much independence and autonomy as possible'. This last point was an indication, despite a stated desire to overcome isolation, of a determination to retain autonomy. This wish had been a feature of the Schools, and was to contribute to their decline.

Following a lengthy period of consultation a second White Paper, *Children In Trouble*, was published (Home Office, 1968). This contained a number of significant compromises, whilst retaining some of the salient points of its predecessor. The first major compromise the new Paper made was to restrict its proposals to those children of 17 years of age and under (as opposed to those of 21 years in the first Paper); the second was to leave the system of juvenile courts intact.

It was proposed that children between the ages of 10 and 14

years would no longer be subject to prosecution as offenders. Instead, if a child committed an offence, it would be possible to ask the court to place him or her in the care of the local authority. Young people from 14 to 17 years of age would still be subject to prosecution but they too could be placed in the care of the local authority.

The powers of the court were to be changed, replacing probation orders by supervision orders and offering a new concept of supervision called intermediate treatment, which in due course would replace attendance centres. The Approved School Order would cease and borstal placements for all under 17 years of age would be abolished. Local authorities were to become responsible for developing a comprehensive system of community homes for children, which would be planned by joint committees of authorities, in consultation with voluntary bodies wishing to participate.

Despite these modifications *Children in Trouble* still contained radical changes to the existing system. The removal of the Approved School Order, the merging of the schools into a system of Community Homes, the setting up of Regional Planning Committees, the changing role of school managers, the idea of Intermediate Treatment, all would have a profound impact on the Approved Schools and would mark a major change in their status.

An editorial in the Residential Child Care Association's monthly magazine, *The Child in Care* , in June 1968 was typical of the general welcome given by the child care worker, both field and residential, to the proposals, 'On the whole a wise and imaginative document has been given to us'. It was also observed:

> *...it may seem positively revolutionary to the heads of some Approved Schools that they will become part of a Children's Department. In reality however, this ought to be seen as the first part of a natural development of co-ordination so that a broad based flexible service widely comprehensive in its available resources can be offered to those in need in a swift and efficient manner.*

This assessment of the likely responses of some Approved School heads was true to a degree but the general response of Heads was better summarised by John Gittins (1968b):

> *Like everyone else I have been studying the White Paper very*
> *closely and one thing is immediately apparent - this is a very*
> *well engineered piece of work. At the same time however, I have*
> *met no one who seems fully to have grasped all the implications*
> *of the proposed changes. I would sum up the prevailing mood as*
> *'rather pleased but rather muddled and hoping that somebody*
> *will tell us how it will all work out.*

It must be acknowledged that there was some cynicism and disenchantment with the new liberal approach from staff engaged in daily dealings with the youngsters. This mood is well captured in a satirical song, *Foresight Saga* by A.J. Henderson, published in the same edition of the *Approved School Gazette* as Gittins observations (Gittins, 1968a). Below are two of the nine verses:

> *In our Community Home,*
> *In our Community Home,*
> *The children are darlings, they're no longer brats*
> *We have little parties and heart-to-heart chats,*
> *And all sit around in White Paper Hats,*
> *In our Community Home.*

> *In our Community Home,*
> *In our Community Home,*
> *They've abolished all evil, no stigma will stick,*
> *No one's to blame for we're all might sick,*
> *You're cured by the time you can say 'Uncle Dick',*
> *In our Community Home.*

In view of the continued rumblings in the Approved Schools Service about the way in which the Court Lees affair had been handled it was hardly surprising that there was a certain amount of ill feeling and mistrust of Government attitudes to the schools by staff.

The Association of Headmasters, Headmistresses and Matrons of Approved Schools (1969) produced a monograph in which it made known its views on the legislation being prepared in the wake of the White Paper, *Children in Trouble* (Home Office, 1968). In commenting on one particular aspect of the proposals it used the phrase 'The writing is on the wall and we cannot ignore it'. This phrase reflects much of the official response of the Approved School service to the developments of the mid and late 1960s. It was realised that a radical change of attitude was to be advocated by Government and some, such as Gittins, accepted there was a need for such change and an opportunity for the Approved School service to develop. Others, however, regretted the proposed changes and, in some cases, expressed opposition to a number of the individual proposals.

The term Community Home in particular incurred their disapproval. It was first introduced in *Children in Trouble*:

'Community Home' will be the common legal description for a wide range of establishments meeting the needs which are now served by local authority children's homes and hostels, remand homes, reception and remand centres, local authorities and voluntary approved schools.

The Association of Headmasters, Headmistresses and matrons of Approved Schools asserted their opposition to the new title, observing 'we are schools and we urge the word 'school' should be included in the generic title, 'Community Homes and Schools' seems to us to be a much more accurate designation of function and to bring out the necessary educational dimension'. They also argued that the changes would damage staff recruitment and undermine their position in salary negotiations which had been undertaken on the basis of parity with mainstream education, with additional special responsibility allowances.

The role of managers and the future of voluntary schools was another area to cause some concern. Under the new proposals there would be three categories of Approved School (or Community Home): local authority homes; assisted voluntary homes; and controlled voluntary homes. The greatest impact of the proposed change would be on the voluntary managed schools (which were the great majority). These changes in the management structure and powers would be contained in 'the Instrument of Management' to be drawn up for each school not managed by the local authority and submitted to the Secretary of State for approval.

In 'Assisted Status' homes the managers would be charged with the task of the provision and maintenance of the home and would be responsible for determining the fees to be charged for the use of the facility to the user local authority. Two thirds of the managers would be appointed by the trustees or other representatives of the founders of the school. The local authority would be responsible for professional oversight of a particular school, within the context of the new Regional Plan, and would provide the remaining third of the managers.

It was also stated in the White Paper that only organisations which had the support of a larger body than their own managing group would normally be accorded 'assisted status'. This would result in locally managed and owned schools having to either go over to local authority ownership or become 'controlled status' schools.

The 'Controlled Status' home/school was, in effect, a device for moving the major responsibilities for managing a school from the voluntary organisation to a local authority, whilst enabling the voluntary body to retain ownership of the property and some share in the management. Under this arrangement the financial responsibility would rest wholly with the local authority. Two thirds of the managers would be from the local authority and a third from the voluntary body.

Under the new proposals managers would no longer have parental rights in respect of the children in the community homes. In future these powers would normally be exercised by the local authority which had placed the child in the school. The Association of Headmasters, Headmistresses and Matrons of Approved Schools lamented the passing away of these powers from managers, stating that the children would be deprived of having someone with personal knowledge of them and a special responsibility involved in decisions about their care. In practice the decisions about these matters had usually been made by the head of the school. The White Paper proposed that it would be the task of the professional staff to make such decisions, within the context of the overall responsibility of the local authority. This would give added importance to the role of the local authority social worker. As a result of this, it was hoped, the perspective of the school team caring for the child would be broadened. The social worker would have a knowledge of the child's life prior to entering the school and would be able to continue to be involved both while the child was in the school and when the child left the school.

The merits of the old system were often illusory, since the only time most managers exercised their parental status was when they chaired the regular reviews of the children in the schools. Often the managers would simply follow the advice of the Head of the school although some did take their responsibilities as meaning a more active involvement in decision making. Some managers also took great time and trouble getting to know each child and his or her circumstances, which enabled them to take an informed part in the review process. Where this happened there was an independent viewpoint which could add to the deliberations on the child's needs and future.

Being able to act *in loco parentis* undoubtedly gave managers an added interest in and commitment to the school. The new system would distance them from any involvement in the decision making about the lives of individual young people in the schools. There were occasional exceptions to this, for example St Peter's, Gainford, Nr Darlington, continued to give some involvement to managers in children's reviews up until its closure in 1984, allowing managers to chair reviews.

There was some expectation that the new system of local authority involvement would permit the interest of managers to be replaced by that of designated members of the Childrens, later Social Services, Committee. They would be required to visit the establishment on a regular basis. Some of the children in residence would be from the local authority which had responsibility for the Community Home with Education (CHE), but sometimes there would be few such children. In practice, however, because Committee members had many other commitments, the amount of interest and involvement they would be able to offer a CHE would usually be much less than that of managers under the former system.

The removal of the semi-independent status of the schools run by small locally managed trusts and committees was to prove to be a more significant factor than the loss of the *in loco parentis* status of mangers. These schools, of which there were 61 prior to the new legislation, formed the majority category. The ending of this status, whilst reducing their isolation, also put the Community Homes with Education in a position where local authorities would, in future, be able to make decisions about their closure. Another very important, but little noticed, change in the management of the new CHEs was to be in the manner of their funding. The White Paper gave the matter one paragraph of comment. The funding would no longer be shared by central and local government, instead the whole cost would revert to the local authorities using the CHE. Allowance for this shift in the costing system would be made through the rate support grant.

Gittins (1968a) recognised the importance of the finance proposals but also expressed concern about the possible effects of an uneven distribution of finance on the service, and questioned whether the White Paper had been intentionally vague on the subject. Whether the vagueness was deliberate or otherwise, finance was to prove a greater difficulty than even Gittins had envisaged.

During the time in which the White Paper *Children in Trouble* and the subsequent legislation was under consideration a number of other developments in local government were also occurring. In 1963 the local government of London had been re-organised. In 1966 a Royal Commission on local government for the rest of England and Wales had been appointed, under the Chairmanship of Lord Redcliffe-Maud. The Commission reported, with major proposals for restructuring, in 1969 (Redcliffe-Maud, 1969).

The Committee on Allied Personal Social Services published its findings in 1968 (the Seebohm Report [Seebohm, 1968]). This Committee had been appointed at the time of the first White Paper *The Child, The Family and The Young Offender* (Home Office, 1965). Its recommendations were very far reaching. A new department was to be created from the existing Children's Department, the Welfare Department and parts of the local Health Departments. The new department was to be known as the Social Services Department and would offer a service to the whole family and the community. The Seebohm Report offered a bold and optimistic vision of a service that would 'enable the greatest possible number of individuals to act reciprocally giving and receiving service for the well-being of the whole community' (Seebohm, 1968).

The Seebohm Report and the legislation which followed led to the demise of the specialist child care officer and the arrival of the generic social worker concerned with the needs of all age groups. Seebohm was fully aware of the proposals in the White Paper *Children in Trouble* (Home Office, 1968) and stated that, with the exception of a few reservations in regard to detail, they were accepted as necessary and desirable; and added that the creation of a social services department should provide a firm basis on which to develop the new service.

The Seebohm Report was to add considerable impetus to the movement towards placing greater responsibility on society to cope with its own problems within the community. Its basic premises were well stated in the summary given in the conclusions of the report. They stated that needs must be met 'on the basis of the total requirements of the individual or family rather than on the basis of a limited set of symptoms'. This could best be achieved, it was argued, by a clear and comprehensive pattern of responsibility and accountability over the whole field of social care with the added requirement of more resources and a skilled staff.

The Approved Schools' heads welcomed the Seebohm proposals as a necessary rationalisation and co-ordination of the social work service, but they argued that improvement in organisation does not necessarily bring improvement in practice (Association of Headmasters, Headmistresses and Matrons of Approved Schools, 1969). In particular the Heads were concerned about the marked trend toward treating children in their home environment. Clearly this was desirable, where possible, but they detected an unwillingness to acknowledge that, for some children, separation from their families was the best option.

Others viewed the future more optimistically. The editor of *The Child In Care* (Residential Child Care Association, February 1970), wrote:

> ...we are moving into an era of family care, care which will be based more and more upon the community...Preventative work will develop in the next decade to an extent undreamed of in recent years - residential work, one forecasts, will assume greater importance though perhaps somewhat diminished eventually in size.

The White Paper on children and delinquency, together with the Seebohm Report, were very significant indicators of the radically changing approach to child care and social work practice.

Other developments occurring during this period also contributed to the climate of change. The first of these was the very comprehensive enquiry into residential care chaired by Lady Williams, *Caring for People* (Williams, 1967). This enquiry was primarily concerned with the training and qualification of people in all forms of residential care. It provided documentary evidence of the appallingly low status accorded to most residential workers. This even caused some surprise in the House of Lords where, in a debate on the Report (July 10, 1968), Baroness Summerskill observed of the starting salary of a Deputy Head in a 50-60 bedded home for the elderly: 'My Lords, £455 a year in a 50-60 bedded home! A young girl in an office can get this pay'. To which several Noble Lords called out 'more!'.

The extremely long hours worked by staff and the poor staff-child ratios was another major area of concern. The position in Approved Schools was marginally better in respect of residential child care staff and much better for teaching staff. However, for the generality of residential workers the situation was often so intolerable that many of them stayed in post for only a short while.

The Williams Report concluded that the most effective way of addressing these issues, raising standards of practice and improving the status of residential staff should be through the provision of greater training opportunities. It proposed that there be a single training course for all residential workers irrespective of the care setting in which they were employed.

This was a radical notion at the time and was given a mixed reception. The proposal was only partially implemented in that a small number of generic one year courses were developed. The idea was, however, to re-emerge in later years as the basis of the two year Certificate in Social Services course.

Another group concerned about the low status of residential child care met in 1968 at Castle Priory College, Wallingford. The group consisted of a number of representatives from three child care associations: The Association of Children's Officers; The Association of Child Care Officers; and The Residential Child Care Association. The text of the Report was written by Kahan and Banner. Their recommendations, set down in what became known as the Castle Priory Report (Banner and Kahan, 1969), was to have a considerable influence on the future development of residential care. The Report laid down a carefully calculated set of guide lines on the methods of arriving at the desired standards of child-staff ratios and proposed the number of staff needed, given a working week of 45 hours.

This was the first time that such a model had been made available for the guidance of employers (mostly the local authorities). Previously most staff had been given contracts of employment which had stated 'hours as required'.

Following the Castle Priory Report the principle of a basic working week was over the next few years accepted. Although this was a long overdue development it had major effects on the nature of residential care, in some instances doubling the number of staff involved and increasing the cost of residential care considerably.

Meanwhile preparations were in hand for the advent of the Community Home. An announcement in the House of Lords in 1967 heralded the formation of the Development Group. It declared that its purpose had been to promote change and development by taking problems and subjecting them to scrutiny before identifying solutions. To this end models were built and publications produced to promote thinking and discussion. The Group began by appointing a small working party in February 1968 to consider the development of the residential establishments for children envisaged in the two White Papers. The working party was known as the Community Homes Project Committee and consisted of three local authority Children's Departments representatives, one Approved School headmaster and three Home Office representatives.

In September 1968 it presented its first report to the Home Office Advisory Council in Child Care. The Committee approached its task by considering the way of implementing changes in three Approved Schools: Risley Hall, in Nottinghamshire; St Christopher's in Hillingdon; and Walsh Manor in East Sussex.

There was criticism that the project attempted to make too many generalisations, on the basis of the study of three schools, about treatment methods for Approved School pupils in all schools. These criticisms, and fears, were answered in subsequent publications by the Group, which became known as the Development Group. In the preface to one of its publications, *Care and Treatment in a Planned Environment*, (1970), it was clearly stated that there was no attempt to lay down a blueprint for all community homes of the future. Its purpose was rather to 'stimulate thinking'.

Over the subsequent 10 years a number of reports on the progress of the Project were presented and they provide a valuable record of developments and changes in the Approved Schools/Community Home Schools. Reference will be made in detail to these publications in Chapter 9. These and other developments must firstly, however, be considered in the context of the legislation that was to emerge from the preceding debates and deliberations, i.e. The Children And Young Persons Act, 1969.

Class of 1949
(St Peter's School, Gainford)

Sport, an area for achievement
(St Peter's School, Gainford, 1955)

Eight

The Impact of the Children and Young Persons Act 1969

The Children and Young Persons Act, 1969 was wide ranging, consisting of 73 sections and seven schedules. Part I was concerned with jurisdiction and procedure by the Juvenile Court in relation to children and young persons who found themselves in trouble and with the various forms of treatment that should be available to them. Part II dealt with regional planning provision and management of establishments to be called in future 'Community Homes' under the aegis of local children's authorities, and with the duties of those authorities in regard to foster parents. Part III was concerned with miscellaneous and financial matters. Although the Act received the Royal Assent on 22 October 1969, the changes were to be brought into effect only gradually over a number of years. As was explained in the Preamble to the Act, at the time of its enactment there were insufficient trained staff and other resources to permit all the changes to occur at once.

The General Election in 1970 brought about a change of Government from Labour to Conservative. The policies of the new Government influenced the way in which the Act was implemented and a number of what some saw as 'key Clauses' (Packman, 1981) were not implemented.

The Act was unpopular with Magistrates, many of whom believed that they were being deprived of substantive powers to deal with juvenile delinquents. The police also thought the Act too liberal. The Police Federation called for the restoration of full powers to the magistrates to send children direct to all custodial establishments and were against the raising of the age of criminal responsibility.

The 1969 Act replaced the Fit Person Order, applicable to needy and deprived children, and the Approved School Order, used mainly for young offenders, with the Care Order. Both groups would now be placed in the care of the local authority.

The Act introduced the term Community Home for all children's homes and Approved Schools. Responsibility, directly or indirectly for overseeing all Community Homes was transferred to the local authorities. All local authorities were required to participate, with neighbouring authorities in a given area, in specific planning of the provision of children's resources. This cooperation between authorities was to be undertaken through newly formed Regional Planning Committees.

More care and management of young offenders in the community was encouraged and powers for placing additional requirements on a supervision order were introduced. These powers were to enable the idea of 'intermediate treatment' as it had been called in the White Paper *Children in Trouble* to be introduced, although the actual term was not used in the Act.

As a result of the Act the Juvenile Court had two overall functions in regard to offenders, one as a tribunal of proof, the other as an assessor of provision for treatment of those in trouble who come to its notice. The Court would have basically two types of case to hear: care proceedings under Section I of the Act; and Criminal proceedings under Section II of the Act.

The court had to be convinced of the guilt of the offender and also be satisfied that the child would be unlikely to receive the necessary care and control without such an Order being made. Ford (1975) referred to this process as 'double proof'. In his experience as a magistrate some courts failed to observe the second part of the proceedings required before making a care order and continued to act solely on the basis of the guilt of the offender in making their decisions about disposal. This was one of the reasons why, in the early years of the Act, the number of offenders coming into the Community Home Schools increased and why, once the second part of the procedure began to be more rigorously implemented, the number began to drop dramatically.

A group of local authorities were required, under the Act, to come together to formulate a plan, for their region, in respect of child care provision. There were to be 12 such areas across England and Wales, and they were to be known as Children's Regional Planning Committees, and directly accountable to the Secretary of State, to whom Regional Plans had to be submitted for approval.

The initial task of the Regional Planning Committees was to prepare and submit comprehensive development plans for a system of community homes in their areas. These were to be based on an analysis of the needs of children and young persons in care and would specify the proposed further functions of existing homes and Approved Schools, both local authority and voluntary. The committees were also to prepare schemes of intermediate treatment. Additionally, it was hoped that they would become forums for inter-disciplinary child care co-operation and communications on matters such as training and research.

The membership of the Regional Planning Committees was drawn from the constituent local authorities, usually the chairman of the relevant committee, i.e. Children's (later Social Services), and the Chief or Senior Officer of the department. In the early years all the committees appointed an additional officer, a Regional Planning Officer, to service them, sometimes with support staff. Most committees also had some representatives of other bodies serving on them. Region One, for example, invited a representative of the voluntary child care agencies. Region Two had representation from the voluntary child care sector, the Magistrates Association and the Department of Education.

The committees usually met in full session on a quarterly basis. A number of sub-committees were appointed to deal with the issues of identifying and submitting for approval intermediate treatment schemes, regional child care policies on observation and assessment, secure places and difficult-to-place children.

Plans in respect of Community Homes with Education (CHEs) and the financial arrangements for them tended to dominate the agendas of the main committee. Most regions developed cost pooling agreements in order to assist in the financial management of the CHEs. These often took the form of projecting the cost per place per year on the basis of an 85% occupancy. This exercise was done for each CHE in the region. Where, at the end of a financial year, there had been a deficit in a particular CHE the user authorities were required to make up the shortfall, and where there was surplus this was refunded to the region for redistribution to the member authorities.

The rationale behind this practice of 'pooling' was well described in the publication *Management of Community Homes with Education on the Premises* (Department of Health and Social Security, 1977). It observed that a distinctive characteristic of the CHE system would be that an authority wishing to place a child need not allow consideration of relative costs to influence choice of placement. Similarly, owning or controlling authorities could be confident that the service they provided to the region would not place an additional burden on their rate payers.

One of the main weaknesses of this system was also noted in the DHSS study but not, at that time, given much attention. This was that the pooling system disguised the relationship between cost and occupancy levels. This weakness was not so apparent in the early years of the operation of the new Act, when occupancy levels were generally high. In later years, however, it became a highly significant factor in the withdrawal of many authorities and voluntary agencies from the Community Home Schools system.

In one of the periodic reports on children's services that was required to be laid before Parliament (the successor to the Children's Department reports from Home Office days), *Social Services for Children in England and Wales 1973-75* published in 1976, gives a clear account is given of the importance placed by Government on Regional Planning. This report recorded that plans for each Regional Planning Area (RPA) had come into operation on 1 April 1973. On that date some 2,236 former Approved Schools, Remand Homes, Reception Homes, Children's Homes and Nurseries, became Community Homes. Because of the complex negotiations with some voluntary bodies it had not been possible to complete all the regional plans. By April 1975 the number of institutions which had become community homes and had been incorporated into regional plans had increased to 2,430.

The 1976 Social Services Report to Parliament also observed that Local Authorities now not only 'think regionally' but recognise the need for inter-regional co-operation. To strengthen this trend discussions at a national level between the Department (DHSS) and RPA chairmen had taken place. This commitment to a regional approach was to crumble rapidly in the 1980s in a manner which suggests some fundamental weakness in the arrangement from the onset. The introduction of regional planning was however, to prove to be far less controversial than the implementation of the legislation concerning the activities of the juvenile courts.

One of the early difficulties of the working of the Children and Young Persons Act 1969 was that some magistrates had convinced themselves (although it was certainly not in the Act) that, when they made a Care Order, the local authorities would accept this as a direction to remove the child from home and make provision for him or her in some form of institution. When in certain instances this did not happen there was some consternation and anger from these magistrates. Their concern was further fuelled when some of those children were subsequently returned to Court with more charges of criminal behaviour.

The Act, however, had specifically removed from magistrates the right to decide precisely how to deal with a child they had placed in the care of a local authority. Local authorities were vulnerable to criticism on this issue because they were not always able to provide either the intensive support that some children subject to Care Orders needed, or sufficient residential places.

Another important development, included in the Act, was the requirement for the police to consult with the local authority before bringing a child to court. This was designed to ensure that all other means were explored before deciding on a court appearance. Similarly the Act laid down that a young person (14-17 years of age) should not be brought before a court for care proceedings unless it was clear that:

...it would not be adequate for the case to be dealt with by a parent, teacher or other person or by means of a caution from a constable or through the exercise of the powers of the local authority or other body not involving court proceedings (Part 1 Sec.5(2)).

The Act, in giving formal recognition of the power of the police to caution offenders, opened the way for a major strategy for dealing with young offenders as an alternative to the juvenile court. Although it was already within the power of the police to exercise their discretion in regard to prosecution of offenders, the 1969 Act gave this an added status and impetus.

Some police forces, for example that in Liverpool and the Metropolitan Police, had already begun to develop schemes aimed at dealing with petty juvenile offenders in a less formal way. In 1969 the Metropolitan Police, and subsequently other police forces, introduced Juvenile Bureau Schemes. Procedures were developed for advising education, probation and social services departments that a juvenile had been apprehended committing an offence. These departments were asked to advise the police of any information that would assist in deciding how best to deal with the young offender.

In cases in which the offender admitted the offence, and the parent or guardian of the child and the injured party agreed, a senior police officer could issue a formal caution. During the period 1971-77 cautioning of young offenders by police increased by 54% in the case of offenders under 14 years of age and 63% for those over 14 years. Cautioning was to become one of the major strategies for dealing with young offenders.

During the progress of the Children and Young Persons Act, 1969 through Parliament the Conservative Party had been opposed to many of the proposed changes. When the Conservative Party came to power in 1970 they phased in various parts of the Act and postponed some of it indefinitely, for example the age of criminal responsibility was not increased to 14 years of age.

Meanwhile, other developments were to have an added impact on the way in which young offenders were managed. The passing of the Local Authorities Social Services Act 1970, (which was implemented in April 1971) meant that the Children's Departments were absorbed into a much larger body, the Social Services Departments, with responsibility for all client groups. Added to this was the introduction of new and wider local government boundaries on 1 April 1974 under the terms of the Local Government Act 1972. This affected 35 of the 45 County Councils. All Borough Councils within the boundaries of County Councils were merged into the new County Councils. In six of the large industrial and urban areas new council structures, i.e. Metropolitan Councils, and boundaries were also introduced.

These many changes caused considerable management difficulties for the newly created Community Homes. It would have been far more constructive for the social services and local government legislation to have been introduced before the Children and Young Persons Act 1969, so avoiding the disruptions in the early days of the implementation of the latter. As it transpired, when the social services departments were brought into being the Act had only been in existence for three years.

Before these new departments had come to terms with themselves and much of the new Act, many were again shaken up by the change of boundaries.

These changes, in particular, weakened the new Regional Planning Committees (RPCs) which had been operating for only four years (and three of these years had been spent preparing for the Committees to begin work). Brian Latham, professional adviser to Region One 1976-1978, stated that the boundary changes made regional planning superfluous in some areas. Kent, for example, became almost self sufficient in child care resources. Ford (1975) predicted that, with more local authorities being able to be self sufficient, the time of the large community home would be over, although some would continue in use for an interim period. He urged that each local authority should try to have its treatment facilities within its own boundaries so that children would not be separated from family, school and the neighbourhood. The larger local authorities were able to do this with the implementation of the Local Government Act 1972.

Throughout the 1970s the Children and Young Persons Act 1969 was criticised by those who saw it as leading to an upsurge in juvenile delinquency. Its supporters attributed the limited impact of the Act in this area to the fact that it had only been partially implemented.

A survey of the working of the 1969 Act was carried out by MIND (National Association for Mental Health) (MIND, 1975). The study, undertaken in 11 local authorities, found that there had been a 25% rise in juvenile crime in four years. Section 4 of the Act, requiring consultation between the police and social services before prosecution of a young offender, had not been implemented. Some police areas had no Juvenile Bureau. There had been greater use of prison for young people, with 4,654 being remanded to prison awaiting trials in 1974. This was partly due to the increased use, by magistrates, of Certificates of Unruliness. It was also found that 95% of Care Orders had resulted in residential placements. The former Approved Schools were being used as frequently as they had prior to the Act. Supervision Orders, the successor to the Probation Order for young offenders, were used much less often. Intermediate treatment had not been developed to any significant degree.

The survey concluded that the 1969 Act had proved disappointing in practice. It was suggested that this was because the Act was based on the mistaken belief that 'care' and 'control' were compatible and that delinquent children should be made subject to 'treatment'. The logic of these arguments was that some children had to be kept in secure conditions but that it was an illusion to talk of 'treating' them. It also urged that there should be increased communication between the police, education departments, health authorities and social services departments. The lack of any systematic monitoring of the working of the 1969 Act was described as deplorable. Finally, concern was expressed at so much local authority expenditure being used to set up new residential child care provision.

These criticisms were valid in many respects, although some of the general conclusions of the MIND Report about the working of the Act were premature, given the short time it had been in force. It was clear that supporters and opponents of the Act continued to be concerned about its impact.

In 1977 a number of social work agencies, which included representatives from the advisers to children's regional planning committees, directors of social services, community home schools, probation officers, residential care workers and representatives from the voluntary child care organisations, came together and appointed a steering group which a year later produced an evaluation of the Act (*Community Home Schools Gazette*, May 1978).

The group noted the contentious nature of the Act, and the general dissatisfaction of both supporters and opponents with the outcomes following its implementation. They considered that the Act, particularly in its truncated form, had made only limited changes to the way young offenders were dealt with. Those changes were mainly procedural and administrative in nature. As a symbol of a battle between competing ideologies, however, where its very existence was perceived as victory by one group and defeat by another, the Act remained very powerful.

The Group accepted that despite its intentions, in some respects the Act had not been effective in dealing with juvenile delinquency. In support of this view they quoted Thorpe et al. (1976) who had suggested that sentences received in juvenile courts between 1969 and 1975 had become more severe, whilst at the same time social work activity and contact had been reduced. The social services Group identified the need for more responses from the social services to police referrals of information about juvenile offenders. It was acknowledged that there was too great a gap between an offence and the official response, commenting that 'At the moment young people can sometimes be forgiven for believing that society does not take their misdemeanours seriously'.

The House of Commons, in response to concerns about the working of the Children and Young Persons Act 1969, appointed an Expenditure Committee under the Chairmanship of Renee Short, to enquire into its operation. This Committee reported in 1975 (the Eleventh Report; Short, 1975).

As was to be expected, a variety of often conflicting views were submitted to the Committee, together with a range of advice about the manner in which the 1969 Act should be implemented or amended. The British Association of Social Workers observed that juvenile crime was more closely related to material and social factors than to emotional and family disturbances. The Royal College of Psychiatrists stated that the vast majority of delinquents showed no evidence of psychiatric disorders. The magistrates and clerks representatives claimed that one defect of the Act was that it failed to recognise that some children committed wrongful acts in full knowledge of their nature and it did not allow for the need to have the consequences sharply brought home to them.

The Justices Clerks Society was the most scathing in its criticism of the Act. The Clerks deplored the parts of the Act which allowed out of court action because the precise nature of this was not prescribed and therefore often resulted in no action at all. It was said that there was a lack of resources, of personnel and accommodation available to implement the Act.

It was suggested that the Act had deliberately confused the distinction between the functions of the court, the police and the local authority and that there was no acceptance of the very real distinction between a child in need of care and a juvenile offender. The Act had also failed because it deprived society of an important part of the courts criminal jurisdiction, namely to protect the public. Overall they considered that the Act operated against the interests of juveniles.

The Expenditure Committee (Short, 1975) seemed to take for granted the continuing need for Community Homes with Education, as indeed did the Directors of Social Services. The Directors, through their Association, complained of the constraints central government were placing on their building programmes. It was urged that heads of CHEs desist from being selective about admissions.

The Short Report (as the Committee's findings came to be known) called for more development of intermediate treatment schemes and urged that urgent attention should be given to non-residential forms of care. It proposed that a juvenile already the subject of a Care Order who appeared before a Court for a further offence should be made the subject of a Secure Care Order. It was also recommended that, when a Care Order was made, the social worker should subsequently inform the Magistrate of what action had been taken.

It was concluded that the major failing of the 1969 Act was that it was not wholly effective in differentiating between children who need care, welfare, better education and more support from society and the small minority who need strict control and an element of punishment. The Short Report strongly recommended that, within the framework of the Act, there should be a major shift of emphasis away from custodial and punitive techniques towards intermediate treatment, supervision and a much greater use of non-residential care, especially fostering.

The findings of the Report were however, somewhat contradictory. Of the total of 40 recommendations made, 15 were concerned with improving and expanding custodial facilities, ten with the development of non-custodial facilities, eight with strengthening the powers of juvenile courts and seven with broadening the possibilities for discussion between the police, social workers and local communities in order to prevent the need for prosecution and to encourage the development of local crime-prevention programmes. On the one hand the Report argued for more powers for magistrates and more use of custodial measures, while on the other it urged a greater development of and reliance on community based facilities such as fostering and intermediate treatment (Thorpe et al., 1980).

The Government responded to the Report in a White Paper (Observations on the Eleventh Report from the the Expenditure Committee, 1976) by trying to reconcile these conflicting recommendations. It undertook to make money available for the construction of secure facilities in Community Homes with Education so as to stop the remanding of juveniles to adult prisons. There was decisive opposition to the use of resources for a massive programme of residential provision and an acceptance of the Expenditure Committee's view that there should be a major shift of emphasis to non-residential care.

Despite the Government's response, discontent with the 1969 Act remained. David Thorpe an arch proponent of the progressive approach, summed up the situation well, observing that it had been anticipated that the implementation of the Act would lead to the end of a penal/custodial system for juveniles and its replacement by a system of care and treatment (Thorpe et al., 1980). It had been expected that there would be a higher age limit of criminal responsibility and that borstal would be phased out and replaced by intermediate treatment. In the same vein, Approved Schools were to be assimilated into a Community Homes system. Thorpe suggested that a new system had come in but that the old one did not go out. One unfortunate, but apparently inevitable, consequence of this arrangement was that children now tended to come under the jurisdiction of the system at a younger age.

As a result pressure was exerted on the 'upper reaches' of the system and delinquents progressed to the later stages of their careers more swiftly. According to Thorpe, this was indicated by the falling average age of borstal intake and the fact that the detention centres and borstals had increased their intake as the result of the demise of the Approved Schools.

A process which had begun in the early 1960s, with a concern to improve the system and methods for dealing with juvenile delinquency, including the Approved Schools, was seen by many in the late 1970s to be in some disarray. Major changes had certainly occurred but deeply held conflicting views about justice and welfare, treatment and punishment, containment in the community and custody, the offender and society, spending and saving public money, the structure for local government, the role of central government, and about the role of the social work and other professions, had emerged. One of the many results of this cauldron of issues has been the erosion and near demise of a system originally designed to keep children out of penal establishments, the former Approved Schools, now the Community Homes with Education.

Nine

From Approved School to Community Home

The Community Home system, introduced under the terms of the Children and Young Persons Act, 1969, came into operation on 1 April 1973. The period between the passing of the Act and the introduction of the Community Homes had been spent preparing for the radical changes to the system. This process had begun in March 1970 with the Secretary of State making an order establishing the 12 Regional Planning Areas. Regional Plans had then to be drawn up and submitted to the Secretary of State for approval. By 1 April 1973 a total of 2,335 former Approved Schools, Remand Homes, Children's Homes and Nurseries were formally made Community Homes. This included 121 Approved Schools, 84 of which had been managed and owned by voluntary groups. (See Appendix A for list of Schools.) These changes had been achieved, both locally and nationally, only after many complex negotiations. It was not possible to complete all the necessary formalities before April 1973 but by 1 April 1975 the number of institutions which had become community homes had increased to 2,430.

The term Community Home with Education (CHE) came to be used, semi officially, to note the distinction between the former Approved Schools and other establishments designated as Community Homes.

Only a minority of the Approved Schools which had been run by voluntary management committees had been managed by national bodies, such as Barnardos. Many of the locally run schools were transferred outright to local authorities, although not necessarily to the local authorities in whose areas they were located. Thus, for example, in Region 1 in the North East of England, Wellesley School in the County of Northumberland became the responsibility of Sunderland Metropolitan Borough Council (MBC) and Axwell Park School in the MBC of Gateshead became the responsibility of Newcastle MBC. A number of voluntary schools elected to go into partnership with the local authorities under either 'controlled' status or 'assisted' status. To achieve these changes in status and to regularise financial matters where a change in ownership was involved, it was necessary for the Secretary of State to make an Order under Section 46 of the 1969 Act. By April 1975 the number of such Orders made was 93.

All controlled and assisted Community Homes with Education continued to have a number of voluntary managers. 'Instruments of Management' were formulated and, in effect, these became the constitution of the managing body under the terms of Section 39 of the 1969 Act.

These changes in the management, and often in the ownership, of the schools were accompanied by changes in the structures of social service agencies and the boundaries of local authorities. As a result the Community Home with Education system was launched into a sea of uncertainty and confusion.

The Home Office appointed Development Group had the task of helping the providers of CHEs with the formulation of forward looking policies. Its publication, *Care and Treatment in a Planned Environment* (DHSS, 1970) indicated a shift in emphasis for the newly emerging CHEs. It was proposed that, in deciding what treatment a child should have, greater weight must be given:

> *...to the background and causal factors underlying his behaviour, although it must still be recognised that presenting symptoms in the form of difficult or anti-social behaviour should also receive attention in the treatment situation.*

Community Homes with Education were no longer regarded as places where most boys and some girls who had been formally identified as delinquents would be sent, but rather as a provision for 'children who present anti-social and aggressive behaviour and whose disturbance is such that it calls for particular investigation and treatment'. Community Homes with Education were to be a specialist resource which also offered education on the premises for those who could not make use of normal community facilities.

This was a radical departure from the former philosophy of the purpose the Approved School, where the emphasis had been on creating an environment which offered a structure allowing for basic formal education, vocational training and 'character building'.

The Development Group Report declared that a Community Home must be seen as an integral part of the child care service and not an isolated facility. It was suggested that there were advantages in introducing CHEs for a mixed population of both boys and girls. It was, however, accepted that for some young people a single sex establishment would be more appropriate. The age range for children placed in CHE would be from eight to nineteen years, though it was considered that individual establishments should cater for a fairly restricted age group.

The transformation of the former Approved Schools into the Community Homes system had a number of immediate effects:

1. They ceased to be the direct responsibility of a central Government Department.
2. Children were no longer admitted from all parts of England and Wales but primarily and, as time went on, often exclusively from the Region in which they were located.
3. The Homes moved from being run largely by independent groups of managers to being directed either exclusively by local authorities or by voluntary bodies with a local authority input into their management.
4. The clearly laid down age ranges of junior, intermediate and senior ended, this by default rather than by direct decree.
5. The distinction that had been maintained between children on religious grounds became far less rigid. Prior to the change of status of the Approved Schools there had been, for example, 25 schools which were almost exclusively for Roman Catholics. A number of these had opted for ownership and management by the local authorities but 18 of them continued to be managed by Roman Catholic bodies under the terms of the Children and Young Persons Act 1969. It was left to the discretion of individual local authorities to decide on individual placements and these decisions became almost entirely dominated by issues other than supposed religious affiliation.
7. The limitation on the number of days a child could spend at home on leave from the Community Home with Education was no longer specified but could be determined to suit the needs of each child (and each Home).

8. Heads of CHEs were no longer obliged to accept into their establishments whichever young people they were sent, since the children no longer came to them as a specific requirement of the Courts.

9. The total cost of placing and keeping a child in a CHE had to be borne by the local authority which had required the child to be in the establishment. The cost per week per school was to be determined by the provider local authority. The 1969 Act did make some allowance to offset this additional cost to local authorities by making extra monies available on a yearly basis through increases in the rate support grant, but this money was not specific nor 'ring fenced' from use for other purposes.

All of these factors played an increasing part in the change in function and status of CHEs, and some of them were major factors in the eventual decline of the system's operation.

Throughout the 1970s there was a concerted effort to modernise the methods of child care (though, less so education), improve the accommodation and, indeed, build some new provision. This period was seen by some as a time when local authority social workers and administrators 'armed with their child saving ideology were prepared to use institutions at a drop of a hat and to spend as much money on building them as they could' (Thorpe et al., 1980).·

Much of the attention of central government and the new machinery of local government seemed focused on residential services. Indeed the DHSS Development Group Community Homes Project concentrated virtually all its efforts on changing regimes inside the old Approved Schools. The newly created children's regional planning committees had similarly devoted most of their energies to the role of the CHEs In all very little effort had been expended on the development of services in the community. It is noteworthy that the Association of Directors of Social Services in their evidence to a House of Commons Social Services Sub-Committee in 1974 spent much of their submission expressing concern about the shortage of places in CHEs and associated problems (see Short, 1975).

Tutt (1974) maintained that CHEs continued to have the often conflicting aims that had been present in the Approved Schools. Indeed, he suggested that some of the changes in emphasis of the new system increased the conflict. These conflicting aims were the expectations that the children in CHEs would receive therapy and treatment, but at the same time be subject to containment and punishment. Despite the changes of terminology introduced under the 1969 Act, for example Care Orders rather than Approved School Orders, Tutt maintained that the basic premise, accepted by both staff and boys, of 'inmates delinquency' continued to prevail. He concluded that residential treatment was failing on the counts of custody, rehabilitation and treatment. At that time, however, he believed that CHEs would continue because 'society needs or thinks it needs such a system'.

It was, indeed, the general expectation that Community Homes with Education would continue to form a major part of the child care system, and staff attitudes needed to change so as to offer a better service. Considerable time and attention was given by the DHSS Development Group Community Homes Project to the CHE system. The project involved the group working closely with three local authorities who were building or rebuilding CHEs; East Sussex, the London Borough of Hillingdon and Nottinghamshire. St Christopher's in Hillingdon was the first of the 'project homes' to be built and the whole process of the development of this new CHE was closely monitored by the DHSS team, the local authority and the staff at St Christopher's. A comprehensive account of this exercise is contained in *A Community Home Growing Up* (DHSS, 1979).

A significant part of the exercise of introducing change into the system, was a series of seminars. These involved senior people in the DHSS, the local authorities, the CHE concerned and neighbouring CHEs. The main issues addressed were the development of the philosophy of a CHE, its management and the day to day care and education of its pupils.

A key person in the DHSS Development Group was Barbara Kahan. She had been a distinguished Children's Officer in Oxfordshire and had been critical of the Approved School system believing it to be too punitive. She worked hard to provide alternatives within the child care service and ensured that for a number of years children in Oxfordshire did not become the subjects of Approved School Orders. Kahan was appointed Deputy Chief Inspector in the Home Office Children's Department with responsibility for the Development Group. When the Children's Department was absorbed into the DHSS she continued the work of the Group there as Assistant Director in the new Social Work Service.

The Development Group was concerned with change and practice development, including changing the former approved schools into more child care focused and therapeutic establishments. A report of the Group's activities showed that:

In the eight or nine years since its inception the Group has undertaken many projects and has produced a long list of publications, of which nine have been published by HMSO and the other are produced informally. The Development Group's programme for 1976 involved work with 1,300 people, including eighty-six English and seven Welsh social service departments, thirty-seven local education authorities, thirty-four probation services and eleven police forces (DHSS, 1979).

It is clear from this degree of activity that the DHSS were investing much time, effort and finance in developing a resource for which they foresaw a continuing need. Their involvement with St Christopher's, the 'project home' in Hillingdon, illustrates well the process followed by the Group to achieve their aims. This Community Home with Education was rebuilt as a replacement for an outdated structure. A number of important principles were laid down in the design of the new building.

It was to be a CHE in which the norm would be living in small groups, there was to be a high staff-child ratio, scope for privacy both for boys and staff (many of whom would be resident), furnishing and equipment were to be on a domestic scale in a generally comfortable and colourful environment. 'Thus the philosophy of the 1969 Act was to some extent given a tangible shape in this building' Kahan told a 1977 audience. The cost of this change of philosophy was not disregarded but, if this new approach worked, 'it will be worth the money'.

The involvement at St Christopher's was spread over the years from 1973 to 1977, beginning and ending with seminars. This was to be one of the most detailed pieces of work undertaken by the Development Group and was to be used as a model for much of its other work. The staffing structure of the new St Christopher's reflected many of the emerging changes in the philosophy of care and education.

The most senior member of staff was to be known as the Principal. This title replaced that of Headmaster. It indicated the move away from an educational model of the management structure. It also allowed for the possibility of a non-teacher holding the top management position in an establishment - something unlikely in the days of boys Approved Schools although possible in girls schools and some of the senior boys schools. The change of title also signified the diminishing emphasis put on the formal educational function of CHEs.

The other senior staff were to be known as assistant principal (social work) and assistant principal (education). These two positions gave full recognition of the two major functions of the CHE and also of the equal importance to be given to both areas.

The post of bursar replaced that of matron. As has been noted earlier matrons often played a major role in Approved Schools. The bursar was now viewed as an administrator and home manager. The position of Matron had involved a management component but had been concerned more specifically with overseeing the health and welfare of the children.

The post of housewarden, with responsibility for one of the five separate units which comprised St Christopher's, was similar in title and function to that which operated in the Approved School structure This was indicative of the fact that there were a number of areas which were carried over from former times. The title of housewarden was also related to its continuing use within the salary structure, specifically for former Approved School staff. This was to be significant in maintaining salary differentials between Approved School child care staff and residential social workers in other community homes.

In an attempt to indicate a view of the role and status of CHE care staff, reactive to the new social services departments structures, those who had been deputy housewardens were renamed senior social workers. The main body of residential child care workers, in line with this thinking, were called residential social workers. There were 15 of them in total for the five units. This number indicates the much greater importance attributed to the child care element in the Community Homes.

The teaching team consisted of seven staff, in addition to the senior posts noted above, to organise and offer education to the total school population of 62 boys. The teachers undertook up to 15 hours a week extraneous duties, thus working alongside care staff some evenings and weekends. This practice occurred in many but not all CHEs. There was a large ancillary staff consisting of: deputy bursar, two cooks, one laundress and one seamstress (both positions carried over from the Approved Schools) and domestic staff (six full-time equivalents).

Two clerks undertook administrative duties, carrying out tasks of increasing importance with the growing number of case reviews and increased levels of written records generally.

There were two night staff, whose role was important but who were often seen only as night-watchmen. Night times could be very difficult in a Community Home with Education. For some boys it was a time to engage in pranks or delinquency (on and off the premises), it could be an occasion for running away or a time of lonely distress. These eventualities were not always catered for when selecting night care officers.

Finally there were two gardeners/handymen.

A total in all of 54 staff (or their full-time equivalent), which in practice meant over 60 people working in the CHE. Apart from the greatly increased number of staff, giving a much higher staff-boy ratio, the other most noteworthy feature of the staffing was the absence of the instructors, who had operated in most boys Approved Schools. This was as a result of the gradual abandonment of the training school concept. Some CHEs retained instructors, in farming for instance, but these were phased out over the following few years.

The greatly improved staffing structures, although welcome, added to the complexity of the task of managing a CHE. As the Development Report (DHSS, 1979) observed of St Christopher's:

> *The problems of managing so many professional staff of different disciplines, and ancillary staff, are very great. In fact they can be seen almost to outweigh the problems of looking after and helping the boys.*

The management style adopted at St Christopher's was described as an amalgam of the autocratic and the democratic. Staff and residents were encouraged to participate fully in the life and decision making in the CHE whilst having to accept that there were some decisions that had to be imposed if it was to function effectively.

A feature of the consultative and participatory concept was the need for regular meetings of both staff and residents. Eight different types of meeting were listed. These were:

- *Boys and staff on duty*   daily   9-9. 15 pm.
- *Boys and staff in each unit*   weekly   1-1. 30 pm
- *Staff in each unit*   weekly $1^{1}/_{2}$ hours
- *Senior staff* (principal, assistant
  principals, housewardens,
  bursar, senior teacher)   weekly   4 hours
- *Social workers and seniors
  with assistant principal (SW)*   fortnightly $1^{1}/_{2}$ hours
- *Principal and
  two assistant principals*   daily
- *Principals, senior teacher*   according to need
- *All staff*   fortnightly

This degree of consultation was clearly time consuming but necessary for a CHE with a large number of staff and a regime that aimed at involving staff and pupils in sharing the management of the establishment.

An area of difficulty that quickly emerged was the role and status of the officer appointed by the local authority to be directly responsible for a CHE. As the heads of most Approved Schools had been solely accountable to their management committees, they were often reluctant to accept that they now had to be responsible to a local authority officer, especially if the person appointed had only a limited knowledge of the problems of caring for and educating a group of disturbed and difficult adolescents. The other difficulty was in identifying an officer at the correct level in the departmental structure to exercise this responsibility. Heads and principals of some CHEs were on a salary on a par with the Director of Social Services. Some saw it as incongruous therefore that they should be accountable to anyone less than the Director.

These difficulties were, in some instances, never resolved and were one of the contributing factors to the unease felt by some social service departments about CHEs. An address given by the Development Group co-ordinator, Principal Social Work Service Officer, Jim Hodder, in 1973 described the foundations on which he believed effective residential care and education in a CHE must be based:

> *...one element in a good regime which should be important is the degree of self-determination and democracy, of accepting the child for what he is, enabling him to say what he wants to say in the way*

he can say it. A feeling of security in relation to boundaries is needed and consistency of understanding (DHSS, 1979).

Hodder also questioned the objectives of education in a CHE and asked about the aim of the education being provided. 'Are we training them for the world outside? Are we giving them a trade-training? If so do they stick to it? Is it what they want? Or are we educating them for life?' He implied that the objective should be education for life. He also questioned the relevance of trade-training to this preparation for the life outside of the institution. Hodder did not, however, pay much attention to the issue of formal education.

At the end of the first part of the Development Group's exercise in 1973 at St Christopher's, Barbara Kahan summed up the objective of the exercise:

The new St Christopher's - represents part of an attempt to re-orientate attitudes nationally, to a task which used to be called 'training young delinquents' and is now called 'caring for children in trouble' (DHSS, 1979).

An area of constant difficulty in the functioning of the CHEs, as it had been in the Approved Schools, was the relationship between teaching and care staff. The change of emphasis to care rather than formal education had altered the balance between them. Kahan pointed out that the homes were now officially described as community homes with education on the premises, and that the boys and girls sent to them were sent primarily because they have personal and family problems, not educational problems, although clearly many also had educational problems (DHSS, 1979). As a result of the changes, some teachers considered their career prospects had been damaged.

The solution to these differences, Kahan had suggested, was the professionalism the two groups of staff shared. Although there was still some debate about the nature of professionalism in education, teachers were in fact nearly all fully trained, which was far from the case with residential social workers. It was social work which was engaged in the struggle for recognition in the early 1970s, with some success. Despite this growing credibility of social work, however, teachers still enjoyed far more favourable salaries and conditions of service than most residential social workers.

When the Development Group returned to St Christopher's three years later, in 1976, it was advised that progress had been made on the teacher-social work issue. Social work staff were taking some part in the individual tuition of boys under the guidance of teachers and teachers continued to undertake duties in the 'house units'. There was still concern by teachers, however, about being excluded from the review and assessment processes. The classroom situations remained challenging and difficult, particularly as the more democratic and participatory processes, which had emerged in the group living situation, were not always easily transferable to the classroom.

The reports from internal working parties to the Development Group made clear that many conflicts and uncertainties had emerged from the multi-disciplinary staffing structures and developing philosophies of care and education that been introduced into the CHE. Interactions between senior residential social workers and housewardens, between housewardens and teachers, and between all grades of staff and senior management was a major preoccupation. The Principal had an important leadership role and set the tone for a CHE. Inter-staff rivalries became much less significant under effective management. The successful pursuit of a common task, coupled with deserved recognition of the value of each member of the team would normally ensure that the differences did not become divisive but rather lead to a cohesive staff team. Achieving this harmony was, however, no mean task.

The activity of the Development Group involved complete staff teams exposing their concerns and anxieties both to themselves and to outsiders. It was at times a harrowing, if salutary, experience for the staff of the CHEs involved. It challenged the leadership of CHEs to face up to new methods of care and management. It raised expectations in many of the staff that a new era was dawning. This was certainly true to a significant degree but it was to be a testing time as well as a time of opportunity. Many of the old certainties were being questioned and some staff were not clear about the ethos of the home and boys and staff alike felt this confusion.

Nevertheless the Development Group continued to tackle the transformation of the ex Approved Schools with fervour and conviction and, in the process, continued to uncover many issues. Amongst the topics that were developed at meetings in many different parts of England were the design of the homes, education, staffing ratios, costs, regional planning, corporal punishment, management of CHEs, admission criteria and local authorities 'rationalisation' of services. Great things were expected from the process of redesigning buildings and the move away from the old 'block school' system. The Reports on the exercises at Carlton, St Vincents, Formby and St Gilberts included a number of pages illustrating the design variations considered at the seminars of 1972, 1976 and 1978.

Staffing implications logically followed from the implementation of the 'small group' concept. The model advocated for staffing structures was taken from The Castle Priory Report (Banner and Kahan, 1969). Prior to this Report there had been few guidelines for determining staffing ratios for child care establishments, largely because few employers laid down staffing structures, and staff in children's homes were expected to work an unspecified number of hours.

In 1972, after an agreement of the relevant trades unions and employers, a circular was sent to every local authority from the Joint Secretaries of The National Council for Local Authority Administrative, Professional and Technical staff stating that 'it has now been agreed to introduce a limited working week for those staff and to recommend...that with effect from October 1972 staff should not be required to work more than 45 hours per week without compensation'. This was reduced, in 1975, to 40 hours a week.

The Castle Priory Report's staffing calculations were based on the belief that there should be a staff/child ratio of at least 1 to 6. The Report identified the hours that staff would be required to cover during a 'waking day', taking account of staff absence on leave, courses and sickness. Finally, it suggested staff requirements in various types of child care establishment of differing numbers of residents. These proposals were gradually implemented by employers and at the same time the salaries of residential child care staff were also significantly increased.

The combined effect of the new policies of smaller units, greater emphasis on the residential care component of the Community Home with Education, a shorter working week, and staff being paid higher salaries was to increase the costs of CHEs substantially. Teaching staff, heads and deputies of CHEs continued to have their salaries and conditions of service negotiated by a sub-committee of 'Burham', thus maintaining the link with teachers and headteachers' salaries in mainstream education. As teachers' salaries in the 1970s greatly improved so did salaries of teaching staff in CHEs. Allowances for extraneous duties and special payments for working in a CHE also increased. Towards the end of the 1970s holidays for staff paid on teacher grades were increased from eight weeks per annum to fourteen, as for teachers in mainstream education. Once again staff costs rose considerably.

Barbara Kahan commented on staff costs in a seminar at St Vincents Community Home with Education, Formby in May 1974: 'Staffing will and should be therefore the most expensive item of any residential community's budget. To cut the cost of this is to economise in the most important area of expenditure and to risk the benefits of much of the rest'.

These views, and presumably those of her then employer, the DHSS, showed signs of changing when, in a conference on CHE management in 1978, she observed that all residential care is expensive in terms of resources and that the CHEs are particularly expensive. She continued by asking whether the child and young person, always got the benefit of the extra cost:

> *For example staff costs are, and must, if the job is to be done well, be high, but how much relationship is there between the high staffing cost and the amount of real individual attention that each boy or girl receives.*

The doubts on costs were made even more explicit at a further DHSS seminar on CHE's later in 1978 when Geoffrey Banner, then Assistant Director of Social Services for Wiltshire, examined the options and priorities for social service departments (Banner, 1979). He said that there was a very real danger of CHEs pricing themselves out of the market in the face of a wide range of demand for services by people in the community.

In the two CHEs with which he was connected the user authorities would be charged, from the beginning of April 1978, £10,000 per annum per child. He said that for this amount his department could pay for one year's intermediate treatment for 100 young people, or for 130 places in priority day care for young children coming from families at risk, or meals in the home on two days each week for 1,500 elderly and disabled people. Initially these considerations were acted upon by a few local authorities, and eventually the vast majority. (For an example of the actual costs and expenditure of CHEs and how pooled costs were apportioned in Region 1 for the years 1980-81 see Appendices B and C.)

In the early 1970s, however, the mood remained positive. Regional planners were predicting continuing, even increased demand for places within CHEs. In the DHSS seminar at St Gilbert's School, Hartlebury, in 1973, the school staff were told '5,460 residential places will be needed for the Region. Based on 90% occupancy, an average of 4,910 will be available, having a shortfall of 550 places' (this was for all types of community home). In respect of CHEs it was stated that 'although schools will have become community homes, demand for this type of accommodation in 1975 will be for 985 places of which 857 will be available, a shortfall of 130 places'.

At a DHSS seminar in the Midlands in 1975 there was still an assumption of the need for more CHE places. The Professional Adviser for Region 5 said that while the predicted need was for 580 CHE places in 1975 there was only 419 places in the region. One of the main objects of the Midlands seminar had been to assist Derbyshire and Lincolnshire in the development of two new CHEs, one in each local authority.

Elsewhere in the Midlands (Risley Hall Community Home) an example was given of the demand for CHE places in the mid seventies:

In the quarter from 1 April 1975 to 30 June 1975 the region had received 104 applications for boys places in community homes with education. By 14 July, 88 boys had been offered places, i. e. 85% and only 15 remained unplaced ...Reasons for non allocation of the 15 were - 3 papers rejected - 1 care authority changed its mind, 6 - no vacancies, 5 refused as unsuitable (DHSS, 1976a).

On the evidence of this type of demand there was little thought of the possibility of decline and closure.

Ten

Creating a Caring Community

The role of education in the Community Homes with Education came under varying degrees of scrutiny at the DHSS sponsored seminars throughout the 1970s. A paper by J.R. Fish, HMI, issued by the Department of Education and Science on the subject of Education in Community Homes is included in the reports of the Carlton CHE seminar (DHSS, 1975a; 1978). He identified one of the major difficulties of educating children in a CHE and suggested how the education should be managed:

> *The length of time an individual may be expected to be resident in a community home may range from months to years. Although the length of stay can be varied according to individual need, it is unlikely that educational considerations will be a major factor in determining it. Hence the planning of educational experiences and courses will need to be flexible and compatible with known time constraints. This will particularly affect the planning of courses leading to public examinations.*

Fish suggested that many individuals might be helped by a short term commitment to a recognisable increment of learning rather than by placement in classes or groups for undefined periods of time.

The Senior Assistant for education at St Vincent's, Formby, commented on what he considered to be the prevailing view of teachers in CHEs stating:

> *The teaching staff saw their task not as being to improve reading, spelling and arithmetic of a boy as soon as he arrived, but rather to arouse his interest and to give him the opportunity to enjoy the processes of learning through creative, constructive activities by means of which he would discover his potential and develop a sense of awareness about the significance of his relationships and of everyday activities (DHSS, 1975a).*

The place of some of the trade training resources in the curriculum of a community home school was discussed by the Development Group at Carlton. In the exercises carried out in 1975 it was stated that the case for carrying on a farm as originally envisaged needed examination. Few boys were likely to become farmers, and to make a profit on the farm might not be easy without the risk of employing boys in too many routine tasks for small reward. By 1978 it had been decided to retain the farm at Carlton, although it should no longer depend on boy labour. The boys and the local community would have the farm available as a learning resource.

These developments were in line with Fish's recommendations that, instead of a concentration on 'vocational training and production' the available facilities should be seen as educational resources which were being utilised as part of an overall programme. Fish recommended that the curriculum should include language and communication, mathematics and science, environmental and social studies, creative activities (music, art, drama), moral and ethical studies (religious education, personal/social education), and practical skills (physical education, gardening, wood and metal crafts).

It was clear from the evidence of the Development Group records and from a report published by the Department of Education and Science in 1980, *Community Homes with Education,* that the role of education in CHEs was in a state of change and development. The greater emphasis on the social and emotional needs of the children had tended to reduce the CHEs view of the significance of formal education. Two other factors that had an impact on formal education were the slow pace of the move away from trade training and the less predictable nature of the child's stay in the CHE, which led to difficulty in preparing for public examinations.

The Department of Education and Science study of CHEs (1980), a survey of educational provision in 21 establishments undertaken in 1978, was a useful guide to the state of education (DES, 1980). In a rather disappointingly short study of 36 pages (including an 11 page Appendix) it drew attention to shortcomings of the system and identified some areas of achievement. It was acknowledged that the task of providing education in CHEs was an extremely difficult one and concluded that it was not therefore surprising that the education provided in CHEs was frequently of fairly low overall standards, in spite of the commitment of many of the teachers. This state of affairs did, however, have to be addressed.

The Report gave examples of poor practice to substantiate these critical conclusions:

> *In one girls' CHE very little appeared to be taking place in the classrooms; what was done was often determined by the pupils and carried out with minimal commitment, enthusiasm and effort on their part and the level of demands made by staff was low. With the exception of remedial work the education programme in this CHE appeared to be fragmented, irrelevant, non-progressive and undemanding; no attempt was made to provide realistic starting points linked with the environment, enthusiasms and interests or activities of the pupils.*

It was observed that in some of the boys' CHEs the long established pattern of trade training departments could obviously result in boys being allocated to meet the requirements of the system rather than to meet their individual needs, although it was recognised that there was ample evidence that most CHEs took a great deal of trouble to test pupils thoroughly on arrival and to place them in appropriate groups.

The general tone of the Report is scathing in its criticism of the teaching of particular subjects. Thus on language and literacy it stated that in only a third of the CHEs were there successful attempts to extend the language experience of pupils across a broad range; in mathematics there was an over-emphasis on mechanical work and little attempt to relate the subject to everyday experience, in science half the CHEs had no substantial course and a number of others taught only a minimal element, partly because of lack of facilities and partly because of shortage of qualified teachers.

There were some favourable comments on the curriculum. It was observed that some CHEs in agricultural environments enabled rural science courses to be developed and outdoor pursuits were 'a strong feature' or 'well developed'. The range of work in these activities varied from basic camping instruction in the grounds to a full range of outdoor pursuits including canoeing, sailing, mountain walking, lightweight expeditions, orienteering, pony-trekking, coastal and deep-sea fishing. Yet even here there was concern that not sufficient attention was paid to relating the outdoor activities to classroom work.

One of the major difficulties for the CHEs was their general isolation from the mainstream of educational provision. This was so despite their links in all cases with local authorities and the fact that many were controlled by those bodies. The Report noted that four of the six girls' CHEs and more than half of the boy's CHEs received no support whatever from Local Education Authority (LEA) advisory services, although in some cases LEA support services were available but had not been sought. This was an attempt to absolve the LEAs of some of the blame for failing to provide the services. It also indicates, although this point is not made in the Report, the lack of structure and clarity in the relationship between the CHEs and the LEAs. In its recommendations the Report rather weakly suggests that a study should be made to see what steps should be taken to 'improve' support from LEAs·

It would have been more conducive to improving the situation if the Report itself had recommended some specific action.

The 11 recommendations of the Report are general exhortations about the improvement of the management of the educational provision in CHEs. They give no specific indication of the value Her Majesty's Inspectorate (HMI) and the Department of Education and Science (DES) place on the service offered by these schools, and show no recognition of the service CHEs may be offering to children who, for the most part, have failed to be educated in the mainstream educational services. They offer no views or vision on the future of children who might need to be educated in CHEs. Perhaps the clue to the Report's approach is the first recommendation, which concluded by stating that any suggestion of closer links with LEAs would have to be considered in the context of any action proposed as a result of the Warnock Report (1978). (The Warnock Committee had been appointed to examine the issue of children with special educational needs). The Report from the Department of Education and Science was written prior to the publication of the Warnock Report but not published until 1980. In the event, as will be discussed further in Chapter 15, the Warnock Report contained little of direct relevance to the CHE system.

The DES Report was, however, a valuable, though somewhat belated, appraisal of the state of education in CHEs after ten years of the work of the DHSS Development Group. It did note that the CHEs contained children with long histories of delinquency and emotional disturbance. A clear indication of this was apparent from information gathered in 1980 by the Heads of the 11 CHEs in Region 1, (the 5 Metropolitan Districts in Tyne and Wear and the Counties of Cumbria, Cleveland, Durham and Northumberland), which gave an outline of the case histories of the young people resident in their establishments (unpublished material). The data from the boys' CHEs show that most of the children continued to have a history of delinquency.

All accounts indicate that a CHE was often only used after other measures - including conditional discharges, fines, supervision (with and without intermediate treatment), attendance centres, detention centres, children's homes and foster homes - had been used and found ineffective. There are also indications that some boys were passed around the CHE system and that a few were moved out of it into Detention Centres for short spells and then returned. Some of the children had very long case histories of difficulty, going back to early childhood. Many had had problems in mainstream schools and some had been suspended. Others had histories of mental disturbance and a few had been treated in special hospital units.

The girls' CHEs also had many residents who had been involved in delinquency, mainly theft. The main characteristic of the girls, however, was the frequent changes in their life circumstances in terms of carers and home bases, and their resulting emotional disturbance. This disturbance was often linked with sexual promiscuity, which in turn tended to reinforce the poor self image many had of themselves.

Bill Utting, speaking in 1978 as the Chief Social Work Officer of the DHSS, identified a very important factor accounting for a child being in a CHE:

> *The intentions of the 1969 Act have been undermined more by a straightforward increase in delinquency than by any other single factor. This increase has handicapped the integration of CHEs into the community home system by identifying them even more clearly as institutions for delinquents. The middle ground that most CHEs occupy between open and closed conditions has undergone a change in its boundaries and it has become increasingly important that the role of CHEs in local*

and regional provision be defined as a community resource and
strengthened (Utting, 1978).

Despite Utting's strictures the fact remained that CHEs (especially for boys) continued to be seen primarily as a resource for delinquents and were therefore considered, by some, to be part of the punitive measures for offenders and, by others, to be a therapeutic resource for emotionally disturbed young people. These varying and often conflicting expectations of CHEs, in addition to all of the other factors (i.e. cost, anti-institutionalisation, past history) contributed to the increasing loss of confidence in the CHEs and a decline in their use.

The DHSS Development Group had made a concerted attempt to move the CHEs away from their former task of reforming and containing delinquents. It had striven to change the attitudes of staff inside the CHEs. It did not and could not change attitudes outside the CHEs. It is questionable whether a major change in attitude to the CHEs was achievable given, as Utting has noted, the continuing flow of young offenders into them.

Community Homes with Education were not generally judged on their efficiency in helping disordered youngsters lead more stable lives. As Denton (1980) observed, children who come into CHEs at the close of their childhoods are damaged. They bring with them wide experience of failure, separation, loss, inadequacy and deprivation of affection. It is unrealistic to expect CHEs always to put right what has happened before, whatever their commitment. Nevertheless, she believed that CHEs could offer young people an opportunity to grow into responsible adults:

Within its prescription the CHE can offer acceptable models of
adult behaviour; experiences of trust; interpretation of past
events; awareness of the needs of others and of self; opportunities
of self acceptance; significant events to enhance status; patterns
of adaptability.

One of the main processes formulated in the Children and Young Persons Act 1969, for bringing the former Approved Schools into the mainstream of child care was Regional Planning. Joan Cooper, Chief Inspector, Children's Department, Home Office at the time of the passing of the Act, summed up the purpose of the regional planning machinery when she later (1977) observed:

It was conceived as a means of planning comprehensively all types of community home... It was a move towards rational planning (a system rather than a network) based on local and regional needs across the whole spectrum of residential care for children cutting across local authority boundaries for specialised needs.

Section 35, sub-section (3) of the Children and Young Persons Act, 1969 laid down that: 'It shall be the duty of the local authorities whose areas are wholly or partly included in a planning area...to establish for the area...a body to be called the children's regional planning committee'. The Regional Planning system and its functioning during the early 1970s has been discussed above. The part played by this system in sustaining and modifying the CHEs is significant in understanding how they functioned. Some examples will serve to illustrate this.

'The Planning Statement' of the West Midlands Children's Regional Planning Committee (Area No.4) in 1979 stated clearly its aims. These were to estimate future need for facilities for children in care and plan their provision, to ensure by annual reviews that the facilities were adequate, to provide a directory of residential accommodation for children available in the region, and to assist the Secretary of State, by reference to all Regional Plans, to assess the national situation of provision. However the evidence suggests that not all the Committees were so clear about their aims, and that few stated them explicitly.

North Children's Regional Planning Committee submitted a revised plan in 1978, and whilst affirming its 'commitment to the principles which led to the formation of Regional Planning Committees', the Committee did not go into detail about its objectives, assuming, no doubt, that they were well established. It saw the purpose of its revised plan as the encouragement of both efficiency and good child care practice.

The 1983 revised Regional Plan of the London Borough's Regional Planning stated that the aim of the plan (rather than the overall aims of the Committee) was to offer a framework of information and policy within which the Regional Planning Committee and individual boroughs could plan their own contributions to meeting child care needs. What actually happened should be monitored and plans and forecasts adjusted accordingly.

Most of the Regions were served by Professional Advisers who presented relevant reports with recommendations for action. The decision makers in the Committees were the local authority members who, in turn, were advised by their Chief Officers, usually the Directors of Social Services. The main areas of interest were the CHEs, as the specialist resources which local authorities needed to share. Local authorities without a CHE within their boundaries depended on neighbouring authorities with such provision. Given this mutual interest, the financing of CHEs was a matter of general concern. This concern grew with the increasing costs, and the pressure on authorities to reduce public spending.

Within the Regional Planning Committee there was firm resolve to maintain the principle that participating local authorities retained the right and power to make their decisions concerning their individual authorities if necessary. As a result there was some resistance to the idea that an independent body, of which they constituted only one part, could make decisions which were binding on them. Joan Cooper (1976) had recognised some of the difficulties when she said:

> *The machinery has creaked a good deal, partly because it preceded Social Services and Local Government reorganisation and was disrupted by them, partly concerns about setting up yet another bureaucracy, and partly through the reluctance of some authorities to look beyond self-sufficiency.*

Cooper, however, remained optimistic that the system would work and would be recognised as a step forward and maintained that it was a move towards a far more rational system than 'the uncoordinated opportunist, adventurous developments, with serious geographic inequalities, which characterised the first half of this century'.

Others were less impressed with the Regional Planning concept and its workings. John Burns, Principal of Kingswood in Bristol, in his capacity as President of the Association of Community Home Schools, observed in 1976 that: 'In many ways it seems to me that Parliament was naive in expecting this new system to work' (Burns, 1977). Although he acknowledged that, in some instances, regionalism did work, he considered it to be an incredibly patchy system. Burns held that the Secretary of State had failed to use his powers even to ensure that the Plans of adjoining Regions fitted together, saying that in some instances Plans were in actual opposition. In practice therefore, whatever the Act laid down and whatever the Secretary of State's powers were, it was clear that a local authority was able to act unilaterally without approval and with no meaningful consultation. Burns concluded that the difficulties encountered in persuading local authorities to co-operate to ensure an adequacy of remand home places during the currency of the Children and Young Persons Act, 1933 had not been heeded and that either the Minister was not willing to use his powers or, in the face of intransigence from some local authorities, could not.

As it transpired the virtual collapse of the regional planning system, once the government had, under the terms of the Health and Social Security Adjudications Act 1983, abolished the requirement for them to exist, was a clear indication of the general lack of commitment by most local authorities to regional planning.

Towards the end of the 1970s, concerns began to emerge in Regional Planning Committees that CHEs had been over provided for in some Plans. In the North (Area 1) Plan of 1978 it was observed:

If occupancy is calculated on a basis of 100% occupancy, then there is a surplus of about 150 beds in boys and girls schools. Calculated on the basis of an 85% occupancy level, as agreed in the regional plan, there is a surplus of approximately 35 beds in boys and girls CHEs.

Area 2, Yorkshire and Humberside, stated:

In 1971 we had (in CHEs) 1078 places with a demand for 994 places by 1975. There are currently 985 places available with a demand by 1982 for 772 places, thus giving an apparent surplus of 213 places. The Regional Planning Committee has agreed to the closure of one establishment with a loss of 58 places.

The London Boroughs Children's Regional Planning Committee observed in its Regional Plan for 1983-88:

There is general agreement that there is an over- provision of places and the Committee is recommended to agree in principle that the number of places should be reduced in 1984 by at least 100; to be achieved by the closure of two or three establishments.

The London Boroughs suggested that among the reasons for the decline in demand for CHEs and residential placements in general were a reduction in the child population, more explicit child care policies, improved preventative services with the growth of intermediate treatment, community service and independent living, more careful scrutiny of the need to receive children into care for professional and financial reasons, earlier rehabilitation of children and continued use of penal disposals for juveniles.

The London Boroughs' Plan, unlike the others noted above, did attempt to take an overview of the child care services in their Region and set themselves a range of objectives accordingly. They wished to redirect resources from residential care to a more flexible range of community services, to increase the proportion of children in care fostered from 30% to 46% by 1988, to reduce the demand for secure accommodation by developing small open units, with a high staff ratio, within the framework of selected CHEs and to use savings from closures to boost training for residential staff.

The other Regional Plans, referred to above, all mention the need to close some CHEs because of 'a surplus of places'. They showed only a limited grasp of the overall development of child care services in their Region. Even the London Boroughs' laudable attempts to acquire this overview failed to some extent. John Ogden, the Region's Principal Adviser, pointed out in a letter to the author in 1984 that forecasts were already perceived as being out of date. The demand for places in regional establishments was now 'expected to decrease further than anticipated because of changing policies at local level coupled with financial restrictions'. The decision as to whether or not a child was referred to a CHE was left, in the main, to the social worker and/or to Assessment Centres case conference recommendations. Later, from the early 1980s, Chief Officers of Social Services Departments had a specific policy of allowing only a limited number of such recommendations or blocking them entirely.

Often the only tangible benefit for a local authority involved in Regional Planning was the system of pooling costs of the

CHEs and access to the Regional Assessment Centres. Each Region had its own particular method of sharing out the costs. In Region 1 North, for example, all local authorities within the Region were, at the end of the financial year, repaid any excess of income from a particular establishment in proportion to the use made of the resource.

In the same way any deficit was met by the user authorities, in proportion to their use. This could mean that a local authority which had occupied only 10% of the 'child days', as they were known, in an establishment could still find itself with a sizeable request for a deficit payment well into the new financial year. This could be all the more galling if, as seems to have often happened, no budget allowance had been made for this 'claw back'. Local authorities who were not in the Region did not have to face this prospect but were charged a standard 25% over the charge for Regional users. In the early and mid 1970s, when demand was high, this pooling system worked well but, as year after year the user authorities were met with deficits to repay, it became far less acceptable.

In 1981 the Treasurer for the North's Regional Planning Committee made this point quite clearly in a letter to member agencies:

> *I understand that a major objection to the present arrangements is the difficulty encountered by authorities in budgeting for a deficit. It may be possible to help authorities by providing them with an estimated deficit based on actual usage in the first half of the year and projected usage in the second. I would stress however that because of the uncertainty of future usage this could only be a guide.*

In the Regional Pooling system for Region 1 in 1978-79 there was a total expenditure of £4,400,158 with an overspend of £350,444. By 1980/81 there had been a dramatic increase to an expenditure of £7,167,403 and an overspend of £876,696. (See Appendices B and C for detailed account of budgeting for Region 1.)

The London Boroughs, with a larger number of resources and generally high costs, showed an even more dramatic rise in their pooling costs (Table 9).

Table 9
Total Cost of Residential Care Provision Offered by London
Region 1973-1983

Year	Cost (£)
1973/74	2,601,307
1974/75	3,942,077
1975/76	5,677,264
1976/77	6,766,089
1977/78	7,649,444
1978/79	8,722,693
1979/80	11,481,276
1980/81	15,259,366
1981/82	17,362,881
1982/83	16,558,162

From data in London Boroughs Children's Committee, Regional Plan, 1983-1988

The London Borough's Regional Planning Report in 1983 reported that the cost of homes within the regional pooling system were a source of great concern. Expenditure on the pooled establishments had fallen for the first time in 1982/83. Nevertheless due to an unprecedented 22% drop in use, the cost per child per week had risen by over 20%. Much of the high costs were attributable to under occupancy. Closures were recommended to assist a resolution of these problems. Figures for 1991/92 indicate that costs overall have been kept down in the London Region to just under £14 million for all regional provision. This has only been achieved by greatly reducing the number of places available so that the weekly cost per place now ranges between £738 and £2,798.

Thus the pooling system, from being a tangible benefit, became a financial hazard. The Local Authorities were all pursuing policies which resulted in a rapidly diminishing demand for CHE placements. The only way of arresting the escalating costs and ensuring high occupancy would have been for local authorities to declare their belief in the value of the CHE system for more children. This they did not wish to do.

The North Region had put forward a valid reason for the Regional Planning Committees continuing to operate when the prospect of closures had first become a serious issue. In 1981 they proposed that an appraisal should be made of each

CHE listing its particular advantages and disadvantages, including the client group with whom it has had most success. Decisions on closure should only be made once this exercise had been carried out.

This role for the RPCs was also identified by the London Boroughs. They did, however, recognise the difficulties in deciding which of the CHEs should close. The Members of the constituent local authorities had the responsibility for making the final decisions but they considered that there no obvious candidates for closure. It was decided to appoint a Member working party to consider the issues and make recommendations about which (if any) establishment should close. The working party was comprised of seven members, made up of the Chairman, Vice-Chairman and Leader of the Minority Group together with four others. It was suggested that the working party be advised by the Committee's own officers, together with the advice of Directors of Social Services and a co-opted member of the voluntary child care organisation. This amply illustrated the number of conflicting interests that Planning Committees attempted to accommodate.

Once closures began, however, local authorities often looked primarily to their own interests and simply announced to the RPCs their intentions, undermining further the value and purpose of such Committees. It was not surprising then, that when the Government, in its Health and Social Security Adjudicational Act 1983, abolished the requirement for there to be Regional Planning Committees with effect from 1 January 1984 that the whole edifice of Regional Planning collapsed almost immediately.

Some Regions, as in the North Area 1, made short lived attempts to sustain Regional Planning in modified form. However, without such arrangements being mandatory it soon became clear that it was not possible to gain the support of all the constituent authorities in any one area. The larger authorities saw themselves as being self-sufficient in most resources; the smaller authorities had few resources to add to any pool and had to cope as well as they could, relying on the availability of surplus resources of their larger neighbours.

Responses to a survey of Regional Planning Committees, Appendix G, showed that the East Anglian Regional Planning Committee was dissolved on 1 January 1984, the West Midlands Children's Regional Planning Committee was 'now defunct' (letter dated 20 March 1984), 'the South East Children's Regional Planning Committee was wound up on 31 December 1983', The Children's Regional Planning Committee for Yorkshire and Humberside ceased to operate on the 31 March 1984 and 'at the time of receiving your letter most of our records had already been destroyed or disposed of'. By December 1986 only the London Boroughs' Children's Regional Planning Committee was fully active.

In the North West an Association of Social Service Authorities planned to continue with some form of inter-authority co-operation. In effect however the idea of groups of local authorities working together to plan services for children had all but vanished in a hostile economic and anti-residential climate. With the collapse of regional planning came the demise of the Regional Planning Secretariat, and its Regional Planning Officers. These officers had often done much useful work in highlighting need, chairing working groups and amassing regional data on a range of child care issues. They were, generally, a sad loss to the child care service.

The obvious immediate impact of the demise of the pooling arrangements was to remove the insurance policy of the provider authorities that any financial losses in CHEs would be met by others in the pool.

The loss of this guarantee served to speed up the closure process. Community Homes with Education were now in the open market and unless their sponsors were either prepared to subsidise any losses or charge high weekly fees they were immediately vulnerable to closure once they became loss-making. What had once been seen as an essential resource in a range of caring and corrective facilities for children and young people was now a highly vulnerable and rapidly vanishing option for impoverished local authorities and sceptical social workers. The loss of confidence in CHEs and the growth of trust in community based alternatives is the subject of the next chapter.

Eleven

Alternatives to Residential Care

The number of children coming into local authority care increased annually throughout the 1960s and 1970s, peaking in 1977 at 101,200 children. Although numbers then decreased the actual proportion of children taken into care, per thousand of the population of under 18 years old did not fall until 1983. Similar trends in the number of children placed in all types of residential establishments (including CHEs) emerge with a fall from 34,600 in 1975 to 13,199 in 1990. Table 10 illustrates these trends.

Table 10
Manner of Accomodation of Children in Care, 1979-1989 ('000s)

Year	1979	1980	1981	1984	1985	1988	1989
Foster	35.9	36.9	37.5	37.9	36.8	36.9	36.1
O & A	4.8	5.2	4.9	3.3	3.1	2.7	2.4
CHE	5.9	5.6	5.0	2.8	2.3	1.7	1.5
C.Home	20.1	19.5	17.9	11.2	10.2	8.6	7.8
Other	33.2	32.9	31.5	23.7	21.0	18.0	17.8

Based on data from the Utting Report, 1991
O & A - Observation and Assessment Centre
Other - includes living with a parent or guardian or in a special boarding school

The peak occupancy of the CHEs was in 1973. In that year there were 7,100 boys and girls in residence. For the next five years the numbers remained well above 6,000 but thereafter they began, slowly, to fall. The pace of decline increased considerably in the 1980s; by 1990 there were only 1149 boys and girls in CHEs.

These developments are explained by a number of factors. There was alarm at the seemingly non-stop increase in admissions into care and concern about the amount of residential provision available to meet this increase. There was also a growing hostility to the concept of institutional care. There was an increasing awareness that community based provision was much less expensive than residential care, and that it was often a better form of care. The loss of confidence in CHEs was further fuelled by evidence that they were not effective in curbing delinquency for the majority of children, a view supported by arguments based on experiments in child care methods in the United States of America that suggested that institutions were now a largely outmoded approach. Other factors in the trend away from residential care were the increased power of field social workers to determine the placement of a child in care, and the loss of authority by the magistrates to specify the type of placement for a child coming into care. There had also been a significant increase in the range of alternative strategies available for the management and placement of children in care, for example, fostering of adolescents on remand, intermediate treatment, and cautioning of offenders. This resulted in residential care being but one of a range of options.

The expansion of the fostering and adoption services began to be seen as the best alternative for children unable to live in their own homes. Thus the proportion of children in care 'boarded out', as fostering is still officially known, rose steadily from 32.0% in 1973 to 41.5% in 1982, and 56.9% in 1990.

The publication of *Children Who Wait* (Rowe and Lambert, 1973) probably marks the beginning of the current emphasis on substitute family care. Rowe and Lambert identified children in residential care who they considered were in need of placement with families. Over the country as a whole, it was stated, there were up to 6,000 children of pre-school or primary school age who were in the care of social agencies and who needed a substitute family. It was observed that 'since adolescents were not very often placed with new parents the study had been limited to those children who had not yet reached their eleventh birthday'. The fact that the study was concerned with the under eleven year olds was quickly forgotten and instead an interest developed in placements for all children of any age.

Kent County Council sponsored one of the earliest projects aimed at finding foster families for adolescents and claimed considerable success in doing so. Its Director of Social Services,

Nicholas Stacey, was amongst the first of those in senior positions to advocate the reduction of residential child care. He spoke of these developments at the annual conference of the Association of Community Home Schools in 1976. A somewhat jaundiced account of his speech is given in the *Community Home Schools Gazette* (Stacey, 1977), which reported that he commended the merit of Kent's own scheme of professional fostering, stressing that it needed to be planned and supported with a great deal of expertise and care. He linked the development of professional fostering to the closure of North Downs CHE, for which Kent had had responsibility, and pointed out that Kent spent £3m per year on 1,000 children in institutions out of a budget of £20m for the whole of Social Services provision. This was 'unacceptable disproportionate'. North Downs CHE was probably the first casualty of this new approach, borne partly of expediency and partly out of loss of confidence in the efficacy of the residential system.

Nancy Hazel and Rosemary Cox launched their professional foster parent scheme for Kent in March 1973. In their prospectus they stated that the aim was to test out how far the treatment functions at present performed by residential establishments for children and young persons could be transferred to persons living in private homes in the community. In doing so they introduced the practice that foster parents should receive a professional fee. Other local authorities and voluntary child care agencies soon began to develop similar schemes.

In one of its later reports, *Community Provision For Young Offenders* (North West Region Social Services Agencies, 1981a), the DHSS Development Group turned its attention from its previously almost exclusive concern with CHEs to consider the emerging community alternatives. There were accounts of 'remand fostering' which started in the Wirral Local Authority in 1981 and involved the placement of young people on remand from the Court into foster care.

There were also reports on 'Contractual Fostering in Bolton', which graphically illustrate the implication of policy changes in terms of reduced use of residential provision and reallocation of finances. Bolton cut back on its use both of conventional children's homes and its reliance on out of Borough CHE placements, from 242 to 161 in the former case and from 51 to 7 in the latter. As a result of this action £378,000 was saved, of which £244,000 was reallocated to employ 12 extra social workers and 20 contract foster parents.

In 1982 the London Boroughs Regional Planning Committee published *A Survey of Special Fostering Schemes in London* The survey showed that on 31 March 1982, eight London Boroughs had special fostering schemes intended for delinquent and disturbed children aged 11 years and over and that the number of children on placement across the eight schemes was 102. According to the information provided the children in placement would most likely have been in some form of residential care, including CHEs, if the schemes had not existed. There was further evidence that the total number of children placed in such schemes by the local authorities could be more than doubled.

Much of the thinking and practice on the concept of fostering for delinquent children had originated in the United States and Sweden. Hazel and Cox (1973), discussed the merits of the child systems in these two nations. In Sweden 80% of children were placed in foster homes and in Massachusetts, USA, there were moves towards a policy of deinstitutionalisation, particularly for delinquent children and adolescents. Both Sweden and Massachusetts had rejected the concept of 'residential warehousing'.

'Massachusetts' became the rallying cry of many who wished to see the demise, or at least a major reduction, of residential provision for young offenders in Britain. Terms like 'decarceration', 'decriminalisation' and 'de-institutionalisation' were used by many who saw Massachusetts as a sign of what could be achieved with a resolute approach.

Joan Cooper, in her capacity as Director of Social Work Services, wrote a brief factual account of her visit to Massachusetts (Cooper, 1976). Her conclusion was somewhat tentative:

> *In short there has been a major shift from custodial and large scale institutional response towards smallness in scale and variety of provision. For historical and cultural reasons the shift in Massachusetts has been achieved through the purchase of service within an existing and well developed private sector. In this country for historic reasons, greater variety exists within the public sector.*

Cooper's conclusions seem to suggest that the situation in

Massachusetts was not directly applicable to England and Wales.

An account of the developments in Massachusetts by one of the main participants in those changes, Yitzhak Bakal confirms that the comparing of the system with that in England and Wales was not entirely appropriate (Bakal, 1973). Bakal was a senior administrative officer of the Massachusetts Department of Youth Services, the body charged with the responsibility of the management of young offenders. It is clear from his full and cogent account of the dramatic developments in Massachusetts between 1969 and 1973 that many of the developments were a mixture of expediency, desperation, and daring innovation against a background of political squabbling, image making and liberal thinking.

Until 1969 the Division of Youth Service (DYS) had been responsible for managing five large training schools and four detention centres. Bakal recalled that the programmes in the institutions were poor. There were no certified academic or educational programmes and vocational training was limited, offering outmoded skills. Clinical services were almost non-existent. In addition, staff members were untrained and unskilled. The treatment inside the institution had been at best custodial and at worst punitive and repressive. The staff used force on occasions and Bakal gave examples of recalcitrant children being made to drink water from toilets, or scrub floors on their hands and knees for hours on end. Solitary confinement was also used extensively.

In response to public and media pressure the DYS tried to introduce more liberal and permissive regimes. When these failed it was decided to take more radical action and make a virtue of a necessity. Thus Bakal records that the department abandoned gradualism: 'During the January 1972 legislative recess Miller used his commissioners discretionary powers to officially close the institutions'. The training schools were fully occupied at the time of the closures. Those offenders who could not be immediately paroled, placed or referred to community programmes were housed temporarily on the University campus.

On the face of it this exercise would seem analogous to the closing of all CHEs overnight; there are dangers however in making such a comparison. In the first place, unlike the CHEs, the institutions closed were used by the Courts specifically for young offenders. Secondly there were residential units, other than the training schools for the young offenders. These were known as group homes, many of which were run by privately managed agencies. In closing the training schools the DYS was divesting itself of the burdens of managing publicly owned institutions, thus opting out of the politically embarrassing dilemma of having to choose to support either a harsh or a permissive regime for these establishments.

Table 11 shows the distribution of young people in the care of the DYS after closures of what Bakal refers to as the 'reform schools'. There can be no doubt that a bold and imaginative change had occurred in Massachusetts in its management of its young offenders, but to say that it had closed all its institutions is highly misleading. It did close most of its own institutions and it did aim at a policy of much greater reliance on community based provision, but it certainly continued to make a significant use of residential care.

Table 11
The Placement of Young Children Following the Closure Of Massachusetts Institutions

Group Homes	500
Private Residential Care	150
Total in Residential Care	650
Foster Home	190
Home +Day Care	600
Total in Community	790

Based on figures presented in Bakal, 1973

In Great Britain in the mid 1970s the anti-residential lobby was gaining momentum and Massachusetts, with its message of 'we closed all our institutions overnight and everything stayed alright', was 'convenient evidence'.

In the early 1970s there was continued concern about the best ways of responding to the problems of juvenile delinquency. The House of Commons had appointed a Expenditure Committee to examine the workings of the Children and Young Persons Act 1969. The results of the deliberation of this Committee were contained in the Eleventh Report of the House of Commons Expenditure Sub-Committee published by

HMSO in July 1975. This Report reflected the somewhat confused position of those responsible for dealing with juvenile delinquency in England and Wales at that time. Community Homes with Education, as such, were not discussed in any great depth, but there was a tacit acceptance that they would continue to play an important role in the future management of young offenders. This is well illustrated by the concern of the Association of Directors of Social Services Departments, expressed to the Committee, about the constraints placed on their building programmes for community home facilities.

To those who argued that the majority of young offenders grow out of offending the Report caustically observed:

> *To say children grow out of crime, however, is small comfort to those who are the victims of juvenile misbehaviour and some sections of the community are clearly unprepared to wait for this to happen. Some attempt must be made both to hasten the process in the case of certain offenders and to deter others from embarking on criminal activities, to contain the hard core of persistent offenders and to punish some offenders. There is a limit to the amount of delinquent behaviour which the society is prepared to tolerate.*

The Justices' Clerks' Society, who saw the developments of juvenile crime management in the USA as a warning to our system rather than as an example, told the Committee that they 'thought that if a level of toleration were to be sought (to offending) it would rise inexorably, citing the American experience as an example'.

The Committee had clearly tried to take all points of view into account, since it concluded by recommending more secure provision and a secure care order for persistent offenders already on a care order , more accountability of social workers to Courts , and urgent attention to non-residential forms of care, i.e. to intermediate treatment, day care, supervision and fostering.

It urged that experiments in fostering disturbed juveniles should be set up in each Regional Planning Area.

This approach, hardly surprisingly, pleased few people. Thorpe et al. (1980) observed that the recommendations relating to custodial facilities and the powers of the juvenile courts were primarily concerned with prosecution and custody as one strategy for managing delinquents, while those relating to the development of intermediate treatment and localised liaison procedures between the police and social services implied a strategy of decarceration and decriminalisation. Thorpe et al. described these as 'contradictory recommendations'.

The Government responded to the Committee's proposals in a White Paper in 1976 *Observations on the Eleventh Report from the Expenditure Committee*. Particular note was taken of the recommendations on residential care and it was agreed that there should be, within the framework of the 1969 Act, a major shift of emphasis towards non-residential care including supervision, intermediate treatment and fostering. The Committee did not actually urge 'a major shift in emphasis towards non-residential care' but rather 'attention to non-residential forms of care'. The subtle change of emphasis is worth noting. Certainly Thorpe et al. (1980) believed that the White Paper represented:

> ...a significant step forward in that it had recommended a shift to non-custodial control; that delinquent behaviour be dealt with locally and that specific criteria to be applied to certain delinquents before they could be remanded to prisons.

Another highly significant shift of emphasis was evident in the way in which residential care was bracketed, by exponents of community based provision, with custodial provision. Thorpe et al. (1980) equated residential care with custody; 'we argue for a policy of 'decarceration'; the removal of the majority of juvenile offenders from residential care, or custody'. Many social workers also regarded CHEs as custodial institutions, not significantly different from detention centres and borstals. This indicated the measure of ignorance and prejudice, due partly to the image many retained of the Approved Schools and partly to their very limited experience of the system following the reorganisation of the social services departments in 1971. As many social workers were to play a key role in the new Community Home with Education system their attitudes were important for its smooth operation. This change of attitude by a number of social workers, social work teachers and criminologists reflected a growing ideological stance towards care away from the child's own home.

Adams et al. (1981) gives a lucid account of the varying ideological viewpoints of those concerned with policies for dealing with juvenile delinquency. Four main strands of thinking were identified, which often overlap: the justice, the treatment, the educational and the social change approaches. The justice approach emphasises the authority of legal institutions and the need to punish or control deviant youth - this was in line with the conservative ideology. The focus is on personal responsibility, right and wrong, and the jurisdiction of the courts. The treatment and the educational approaches fit most readily into the liberal ideology, given prominence in the policy developments of the 1960s. The treatment approach, which has strongly influenced the developments of the social work profession, has been based primarily on the concept of individual or social pathology. The educational approach emphasises the normal processes of maturation, which need to be nurtured and stimulated. Finally, Adams argues that the social change approach is based on the belief that there needs to be radical change in the way in which society is ordered, suggesting that the roots of crime lie in the structure of society.

Adams also noted the concern of radical thinkers with the 'welfare' and 'child saving' approach. He quoted the group 'Justice For Children', which observed that:

> *...judicial impartiality and fairness, especially in sentencing, have been severely hindered by the welfare approach. There is also an increasing body of opinion which believes that 'treatment' can have a negative effect on a child and his family.*

Thorpe et al. (1980) had noted that the whole concept of welfare and the institutions which are supposed to administer it 'have been enthusiastically assailed by advocates of the labelling perspective, radical deviancy theorists and their influential Marxist successors'.

In the context of these conflicting views of juvenile delinquency, and the concerns for economic restraint, the CHEs began to be subject to increasing scrutiny. As Adams et al. (1981) shrewdly observed, 'Wherever professional conviction coincides with the direction dictated by financial constraints, it always proves a powerful combination'.

The success of the vociferous body of opinion dismissing the contribution of the CHEs to the juvenile justice system is demonstrated by the Report of the Parliamentary All-Party Penal Affairs Group (1981). This study contained no consideration of the role of CHEs in any future provision. It was dismissive of residential care, quoting a number of studies (Clarke and Cornish, 1975; Thorpe et al., 1976) to demonstrate the failure of residential care to curb reoffending. The study also observed that 'there has been a sharp rise over the years in the rates of recorded crime among young people'.

A debate in Parliament on crime (July 1986) indicated that this was a matter of concern to all political parties. The chief opposition spokesman on home affairs was clearly reflecting general concern, while at the same time attempting to embarrass the Conservative Government, when he said 'a black cloud of lawlessness hung over Britain today and the country is suffering the worst crime wave ever known'. To substantiate his claim he pointed out that in the last seven years theft had risen by 30%, violence against the person by 42%, burglaries by 52% and criminal damage by 73%.

The Home Office British Crime Survey of 1984, based on interviews with 11,000 people showed that half the women interviewed said they avoided going out alone at night. In 1983 there were 19 attempted or actual break-ins per 100 homes on the poorest council estates. Two-thirds of the incidents in the survey were unrecorded by the police. The 'clear up rate' for crime had generally been declining. The National Association for the Care and Resettlement of Offenders (NACRO) in a paper on 'Burglary' (1985b) noted that 'the clear-up rate for burglary is low, 28% of recorded offences in 1984 and has been going down - in 1974 it was 34%'. It also noted that '69% of those found guilty and cautioned were young offenders (under 21); 30% were juveniles (under 17), a higher proportion than for any other offence category'.

The trend, however, has been to play down these concerns and even use selective statistical figures to, consciously or unconsciously, distort the actual overall picture in respect of juvenile delinquency. NACRO (1985a) observed that the number of 'known' juvenile offenders was 10% lower in 1983 than in 1974 and that the rates of offending had levelled off or declined since 1982 for all age groups except females aged 14 to 16 years. These figures refer to apprehended offenders.

They ignore the fact that the crime rates continue to rise, that the number of offenders caught has dropped, and that many offences are not reported to the police. Clearly the attitudes of those concerned with the growth of crime and the management of juvenile delinquents are influenced by their particular area of concern: for example the police are concerned with the wellbeing and security of society as a whole; whereas for others, for example, social workers, worries about labelling and punishing children prevail.

The Association of Directors of Social Services (ADSS) (1985) observed that the picture was one of a juvenile justice system which has no clear philosophy, and which makes children pawns in a struggle between competing objectives. They believed that the ideals of justice and welfare are not contradictory and ought indeed to be complimentary and mutually embracing. Tutt (1982) summed up the situation well, when he suggested 'that in the conflict of approach to juvenile delinquency, justice versus welfare, ideology becomes more significant than empirical evidence'.

Tutt observed also that the decline in the use of care orders was radically affecting the residential provision of local authorities. In 1971, when there were approximately 7,500 young people, boys and girls, in open CHEs, there were less than 100 long-term secure places for young people in the CHEs. With the decline in the number of CHEs long-term secure places have increased rapidly and, in proportional terms, dramatically; in 1980 some 300 long-term places in security were provided for children and young people. These figures exclude the growing numbers of young people in security in prison department establishments (Borstal and junior detention centres). This apparent concern about the demise of care order placements and the growth of custody alternatives does not seem consistent with the work of the Centre of Youth, Crime and Community at Lancaster University (in which Tutt played a major role) which, among other things, has acted as a consultant to local authorities advising on methods of reducing care orders.

Thorpe et al. (1980) described CHEs, as 'custodial institutions' and claimed that the majority of children had been placed in them unfairly, 'not just unnecessarily and damagingly'. He stated that most children in CHEs were there as a result of a ruling of the Court under Section 7(7) of the Children and Young Persons Act, 1969. This enabled the Court to make a child subject to a care order as a direct response to a criminal offence. It is argued that the children placed in care under this Section were placed against the true spirit of the 1969 Act as stated in Section 1(2) of that Act. Courts have used

Section 7(7) of the Act thus avoiding the application of the criteria set out in Section 1(2). If, the argument runs, the criteria of Section 1(2) were applied, then the majority of young delinquents would not have had care orders imposed on them. The additional criteria set out in Section 1(2) of the Act states that the Court must also be satisfied that the child is in need of care or control which he or she is unlikely to receive unless the Court makes an order under this section.

Thorpe and the Lancaster Centre devised their own criteria to test the validity of the 'care and control' rider when applied to the Section 7(7) cases. These asked:

Is the child a danger to himself and/or his community? Does the child have a home in the community which can, with appropriate support, provide an adequate degree of care and control? Does the child have any specific medical, educational, vocational or psychiatric needs which can be dealt with only in a residential context?

These guidelines do not appear to be entirely consistent with the use of the terms 'care and control' in the Act. In the earlier part of Section 1(2) care is described in terms of, amongst other things, ensuring that the proper development of the child is not being avoidably prevented or neglected, control as not being beyond the control of his parent or guardian. Thorpe's 'care and control' criteria seem therefore artificially narrow. There is no consideration of the absence of consistent interest in and care for a child, nor is there any reference to break- down in family relationships in the child's own home or to a loss of control in a children's home or foster placement.

By using their check list Thorpe and associates were able to 'demonstrate' to three local authority social services departments that between 70.5% and 90% of groups of children committed to care under the terms of Section 7(7) of the Act would not have been so committed had their criteria been applied to them. Whilst Thorpe was right to challenge the growth of the practice of placing children in care via the Section 7(7) provision, there is insufficient evidence that the check list was an adequate measure of the appropriateness of that decision or that children and young people in CHEs were wrongly placed. Indeed case histories in a survey of children in the North Region CHEs, carried out in 1980, record long chronicles of disturbed and difficult behaviour and multiple failures of alternative measures and suggest that the children were rightly placed under the terms of the Children and Young Persons Act 1969.

Thorpe et al. (1980), however, concluded that Community Homes with education:

> *...far from preventing delinquent careers actually promote them, at eventual considerable cost to both the community and the individual delinquent and that moreover, such provision and expense often prevented the development of vital intermediate treatment services.*

Intermediate treatment is described in the report of the Parliamentary All-Party Penal Affairs Group (1981) as a way of reducing delinquency:

> *...by involving young people in constructive activities, offering them opportunities for achievement, improving their social skills, bringing them into contact with mature adults who can exercise a positive influence on them, providing counselling both individually and in groups and involving parents of delinquents in taking more responsibility for their children's behaviour.*

All of these ambitious objectives were to be achieved in sessions of normally a few hours, two or three evenings a week over a limited period of usually months, although in the early days of the development of intermediate treatment schemes there were sometimes more intensive sessions in residence for a week or two. There are still some schemes that involve children in weekend or sometimes longer sessions but the trend in recent years has been toward day attendances only.

Intermediate treatment began after the Children and Young Persons Act 1969 and was to be understood in a variety of ways. Many saw it as having a role in both the prevention and the treatment of delinquency. As a result much energy was spent in trying to determine where the balance should lie between intermediate treatment as a treatment and as a preventative measure. The Department of Health and Social Security *Guide to Intermediate Treatment* (DHSS, 1972) did not mention delinquency and even in 1974, Joan Cooper, Director of the DHSS Social Work Service, was still lending her authority to a very generalised, if not amorphous, interpretation of the concept (as cited in Adams et al., 1981):

*Intermediate treatment is intended for a whole age range from
0-18 years. Within it can be encompassed an informal 'play
group' for an 'at risk' 3 year old under supervision or an
opportunity for motor repair work in a group for a 16 year old
traffic offender.*

Perhaps because of this somewhat muddle-headed approach,
intermediate treatment was slow to develop into a real option
for magistrates to use when placing supervision orders on
delinquents.

Adams et al. (1981) observed that 'many local authorities
relied almost entirely on the goodwill and enthusiasm of social
workers to provide it (intermediate treatment) in their spare
time'. He provided some useful data on the number of young
people involved in intermediate treatment. Reference is made
to an estimate by the National Youth Bureau of 20,000- 25,000
young people being involved in intermediate treatment during
the year ending March 1979. Only one in six was actually
subject to an intermediate treatment requirement, though up
to two thirds were on some kind of Court order, usually plain
supervision. It was also noted that the planned total
expenditure on intermediate treatment by local authorities at
the year ending March 1980 was £4.5 million, although hidden
extra expenses probably took the amount to well over £5
million. As for the staffing of intermediate treatment it was
calculated that by the middle of 1979 there were about 650
specialist staff in the United Kingdom and that 84% of those
engaged in intermediate treatment were usually social workers
with caseloads. These figures are a clear indication of the
relatively slow growth, low expenditure and inadequate
planning of the use of intermediate treatment as a significant
alternative to residential care.

Intermediate treatment continued, however, to grow in the
estimation of social work departments as a preferred option to
residential care for many young offenders. An example of the
reasoning of departments is given in a DHSS Report (North
West Region Social Services Agencies, 1981b). Trafford Social
Services Committee was advised by its officers that residential
placements can reinforce delinquent attitudes and that
discharge from residential care broke the relationship with the
residential worker at a critical time for the young person.
Moreover, residential care was extremely expensive. The

annual cost to the department of maintaining 83 offenders in residential institutions was £340,000 and Community Home with Education placements were, at the time, costing £11,513 per year per child. The cost per place at the proposed intermediate treatment day centre, based on eight children and allowing a staff/child ratio of 2/1 would be £5,933. The centre would provide a specialist intensive method of social work, incorporating education over a period of 12-18 months for 14-16 year olds. The children would attend the centre four days a week and spend Fridays either in ordinary school or in work experience. There were persuasive arguments for most social service committees.

By 1984/5 with the closure of many CHEs and with additional Central Government support, expenditure on intermediate treatment according to the National Youth Bureau, had grown to £19,730,000. Although this was a substantial increase on expenditure in the 1970s it did not reflect either the amount of money saved by the closure of CHEs or the growing need for extra measures as a result of the continuing growth in delinquency.

Arguments about the effectiveness and nature of intermediate treatment continue. Denne and Peel (1983), reported on a comparison of the offending careers of young people placed in CHEs and those placed on intermediate treatment from the Wakefield area. The researchers concluded by claiming that 'on the basis of this study, the transfer of resources from residential care to the intermediate treatment sector appear fully justified'.

Yet the findings did not necessarily make it clear that this claim was justified. The main benefits suggested were that only 67% of the intermediate treatment sample reoffended, compared with 79% of the CHE sample. Denne and Peel (1983) also recorded that, in both samples, 40% reoffended during placement. Two very significant facts were given little attention. Firstly the average length of placement in a CHE was 18.3 months while on intermediate treatment it was only 7.7 months and secondly that whilst only 9% of reoffenders in CHEs went to detention centres, borstal or prison, 23% on intermediate treatment were sent to penal establishments (see Table 12).

Others, equally committed to the 'care in the community' approach have a less positive view of intermediate treatment.

Table 12
Reoffending Rates: Comparisons of Boys on Intermediate
Treatment (IT) and Those in Community Homes with Education
(CHE), 1982

Reoffending	IT	CHE	
	%	%	
After Discharge	67	79	
During Placement	40	40	
Sent to Custody	23	7	

Based on Information in Denne and Peel, 1983

Stevens and Crook (1986) claim that 'Intermediate Treatment is to become the 'lame duck' of the juvenile criminal justice system'. Despite the replacement of social skills training and outdoor pursuits with new approaches under slick headings such as 'heavy end', 'offending work', 'the correctional curriculum', 'tracking' and alternatives to custody 'projects' and 'schemes', confusion remains and the phrase 'Intermediate Treatment' has become a convenient label for a 'rag bag' of social work approaches. Stevens and Crook conclude that 'after 17 years, intermediate treatment is a concept with no useful role to play in the management of the juvenile criminal justice system in England and Wales'. Their local authority, Northampton, has rejected intermediate treatment since 1983 'in favour of a strategy of corporate action, planning, efficient management and monitoring', which also sounds rather nebulous.

Thorpe et al. (1980) have also expressed scepticism towards the 'welfare approach' in the use of intermediate treatment. They suggested that preventing delinquency is not a matter of singling out hapless children at random from disorderly families and setting up what amounts to adolescent playgroups. Rather, they argue, good social work practice with juvenile offenders consists of developing carefully researched strategies with both communities and individuals with very specific objectives and practical actions in mind.

Much store is set by central government on intermediate treatment as a viable option to residential care. The 'All Party' report of the Parliamentary All-Party Penal Affairs Group (1981) observed that the Director of Social Services for Essex had said that the closure of a Community Home with Education in Chelmsford had saved the authority the gross sum of £400,000 per annum and that 'closure provides a real incentive to look at alternative forms of care of a non-custodial nature'.

The 'All Party' group also reported the observations of Sir George Young, an Under-Secretary at the DHSS at the time, (February 1981):

> *At present the development of I.T. (intermediate treatment) is too patchy. Some areas can boast a wide range of activities provided from a variety of sources; in others almost no facilities are available. Everywhere, I.T. at the 'heavier' end - that is for youngsters convicted of more than just petty crimes and beyond the reach of many programmes - is very sparsely available.*

'Intermediate Treatment' is a grand sounding term and under its umbrella some imaginative schemes for young offenders have been developed. Many more ill defined schemes have also emerged with little or no assessment of their efficacy. There is much to support the critics of intermediate treatment and it may be that by its generalist approach, more damage than good has been done to the cause of effectively managing young offenders in the community.

Getting a positive image:
Girls and staff, including the author (centre with beard) at Benton Grange School at the end of the 1970s

Good order and discipline being practised
(Benton Grange School in the 1960s)

Twelve

Diversion and Custody

While fostering and intermediate treatment schemes have played an important role in the declining use of residential care for young offenders, by far the most significant development has been the practice of diversion of young delinquents from the courts. The Report of the Parliamentary All-Party Penal Affairs Group (1981) accepted the view that all the available evidence suggested that juvenile offenders who could be diverted from the criminal justice system at an early stage in their offending would be less likely to reoffend than those who become involved in judicial proceedings. The Penal Affairs Group also supported the findings of the Black Report (Black, 1979) on legislation and services for children and young people in Northern Ireland. The Black Report, found that once a child has been labelled a delinquent, then it is more likely that the child will see him or herself as such, and will associate with kindred spirits, become a focus of attention for the police, and so become stereotyped.

The extent of the growth of the practice of diversion of young offenders from Court in many parts of England is evident from the extensive activities undertaken under the direction of the National Association for the Care and Resettlement of Offenders (NACRO) between 1982 and 1985. In 1982 NACRO created a Juvenile Crime Unit, financed by a grant from the Department of Health and Social Security, to help to bring about a more co-ordinated local response to juvenile crime and offenders in a number of cities in England. The manner in which NACRO went about these tasks, the principles it espoused and the outcome of its deliberations, resulted in a unique and highly significant change of approach in methods for dealing with juvenile delinquents.

NACRO formed Joint Consultative Groups in ten cities or urban areas: Manchester, Leeds, Sheffield, Coventry, Teesside (Middlesbrough and Stockton), Liverpool, Newham (London Borough), Sunderland, Reading and Hull. In each of these areas NACRO invited membership of the Groups from the statutory and voluntary sector agencies with interests in juvenile crime. These Groups eventually produced written reports, published separately by NACRO between 1984 and 1986 with a final report in 1987 (NACRO, 1984; 1985c-g; 1986; 1987). Each of the ten NACRO Groups were given the task of making recommendations with a view to reducing the number of juveniles who come to the attention of the police for offending, limiting the number of juveniles brought before the court and reducing the number of juveniles being removed from home into custody or residential care.

These objectives were based on the beliefs that residential care and custody were equated; that both were generally ineffective and expensive; that bringing a child or young person before the courts was normally unhelpful and often damaging and that the community in which the young person is living is the best place, with few exceptions, in which to tackle the issue of juvenile delinquency. These points became almost articles of faith for the NACRO Consultative Groups and their members. Indeed, in NACRO's final report the point was made that there had been no minority reports and very few dissenting voices (NACRO, 1986).

Despite efforts to ensure that the consultative groups were representative of all concerned with juvenile delinquency it is significant that only in two Groups were there any members directly involved in residential child care, and none of the Groups involved anyone employed in custodial establishments for young offenders. The Teesside Review (NACRO, 1985g) summed up the overall approach well, stating that the prosecution of juvenile offenders should be avoided as far as is compatible with the protection of the public and the rights of the offender. They also held that juveniles should not be reported to the police for minor offences which can be properly dealt with informally. It was urged that juveniles should not normally be prosecuted unless they had previously been cautioned. All offenders under 17 years of age who admitted the offence(s) complained of should be given the benefit of a formal caution on at least one occasion, and preferably also for subsequent offences of a minor nature.

This approach is a clear indication of the commitment of those involved with young offenders, from the police to social workers, to avoiding, if at all possible, the bringing of the young person before the courts.

If informal methods of diversion fail then the police powers of caution are now extensively used. The guidelines issued by the Home Office (1985) indicate the criteria for a police caution: the available evidence must be such as to support a prosecution in normal circumstances; the juvenile must admit the offence; and the parent or guardian must agree to a caution being administered. The guidelines also state:

...it will generally be appropriate for a caution to be administered in formal circumstances at a police station in the presence of the parents or guardian by a police officer in uniform. The officer should normally be of the rank of inspector or above.

There are advantages to using the cautioning process other than the presumed benefit to the young offender.

The Newham Review (NACRO, 1985f) pointed out that bringing juveniles to court for an alleged offence is a complex, lengthy and costly process which normally involves the police in consultation with social services, probation, education welfare services and the office of the clerk of the justices. The Liverpool Review (NACRO, 1984) also noted that 'it is extremely cost effective to divert an erring youngster from appearing in court'.

In *Time For Change* (NACRO, 1987), NACRO records that the proportion of juveniles cautioned rose from 35% of all 10-13 year olds in 1968 to 82% in 1985 and from 10% of all 14-16 year olds in 1968 to 59% in 1985. The cautions are issued not only for first or even second offences. The Sunderland Review (NACRO, 1985c) observed that the regularity of the cautioning system resulted in most juvenile offenders being cautioned twice, and many three or four times before being brought before a court and help offered. In some areas, including Sunderland, efforts were being made to ensure that guidance and assistance were offered at an earlier stage in the cautioning process.

Cautioning does seem an effective way of dealing with most young offenders, if the evidence from Humberside is typical. The Hull Review (NACRO, 1985d) stated that 75% of first-time offenders cautioned in 1982 had not r offended within two years.

Cautioning first-time non-serious offenders is clearly a reason the course of action in most instances. What should be of concern is that the system can become discredited, both in terms of justice and welfare if it is repeated too frequently. It could be argued that instead of enabling some children to avoid being drawn into criminality, multiple cautioning may in fact lead to more offending, since once young people become aware that their delinquency will result in nothing more than a caution, there is little deterrence to further offending. In addition, multiple cautioning with no social work intervention may mean that welfare matters, such as lack of parental interest or control, may not be investigated until the young person has become an habitual offender.

If a young person does eventually reach the Courts, the NACRO studies proposed that the practice of preparing social enquiry reports, for first time offenders at least, should cease. This is because, it is said, too many social work reports recommend care or custody. This view suggests doubts about the judgement of social workers and a fear that the Courts can make harsh decisions too hastily.

The whole process of attempting to respond to, and, where thought necessary, deal with young offenders in the community calls for a high degree of liaison, communication and agreement between various agencies, such as the police, social services, educational services, health services, community groups and voluntary bodies. Such co-ordination, as the NACRO studies themselves illustrated, is no easy task. It should be noted that NACRO had paid employees acting as co-ordinators in all of these exercises. Getting all relevant bodies to meet and co-ordinate their responses was one of the prime objectives of the NACRO Groups. The Reading Group (NACRO, 1985c), identified one of the problems of such a wide spread of responsibility in the groups when it observed:

> *...there is not a uniform method of keeping information that is used to devise policy by all relevant agencies which is easily accessible by them, within the bounds of confidentiality.*

Co-ordination responsibilities, joint decision making processes and sharing information are not insuperable tasks but they do rely on much good will and careful management and failure in these areas is not always immediately apparent. This must surely be a major concern with the growing reliance on an ad hoc community care system and with a virtual run-down of specialist residential provisions.

In view of the complete lack of attention given to the merits of residential care in the NACRO urban delinquency studies, it comes as something of a surprise to discover that their policy review for a new framework of response, *Time For Change* (NACRO,1987), recommends:

> *Appropriate residential provision managed by local authorities, not the Home Office, could form part of a range of supervisory measures available for the small proportion who must still be detained.*

The Report also suggests the creation of regional facilities, 'organised on a similar basis to the former pooling system'.

The general movement to encourage and facilitate communities to deal with their young delinquents must be welcomed. The fear is, however, that some unrealistic expectations, both about the capacities of these communities to respond and to tolerate more than a certain level of offending, will lead to an overburdening of this system, resulting in a state of lawlessness or even occasional complete breakdowns in law observance, as has been witnessed in inner city riots in Liverpool, Birmingham, Manchester, Tyneside and parts of London, spasmodically from 1981 onwards.

Bakal (1973), when writing of the Massachusetts episode, argued that it was necessary to apply what he called the 'Shotgun Approach to Change'. He suggested that it was only when old methods were abandoned that, of necessity, new options had to be developed. This seems to be a precarious manner in which to develop a policy for managing delinquency and young delinquents. Community based responses for delinquency demand careful planning and clear structures if they are to avoid collapse.

In spite of all the effort to divert young offenders from courts, from reception into care and from CHEs, the greatest percentage increase in methods used for managing young offenders has been in the penal system. Between 1969 and 1977 the number of juveniles sent to detention centres went up by 158% from 2,228 to 5,757. In the same period borstal sentences rose by 136% from 818 to 1,935. As the turnover in penal establishments is fairly frequent the actual number of young offenders at any one time is not as great as the figures given above.

The Report of the Parliamentary All-Party Penal Affairs Group (1981) referred to a speech made by the then Home Secretary, Leon Brittan, on 16 November 1979 in which he observed:

During the past twenty years, the proportion of convicted adults received into custody has been more than halved. During the same period the proportion of juveniles receiving custodial sentences...has more than tripled. In 1955 an adult was 20 times more likely than a juvenile to get a custodial sentence for an indictable offence. Now he is only twice as likely.

Despite recording these remarks the 'All Party' Report did not examine a possible role for Community Homes with Education as an alternative to custody.

Because of the continued Government concern about the growth in crime new legislation was put before Parliament. The Criminal Justice Act 1982 was introduced, amongst other things, to add to the power of magistrates to deal more effectively with young offenders. The Act abolished sentences of borstal training and imprisonment for offenders under 21 and replaced them with youth custody orders. Magistrates were empowered to make such orders, previously only Crown Courts could send offenders to borstal.

Shorter detention centre orders, from between 4 months to 21 days, were also introduced. It became possible to levy fines on parents of offending juveniles. A 'Charge and Control Order' allowing the Court to require a local authority, when the child is already in care, to be removed from home, was also introduced. A night restriction (curfew) could be imposed for up to 30 days. Clearer and more strictly defined procedures for placing children in secure accommodation were laid down. The Act also established tighter criteria for placing a child in care when he or she was an offender. The majority of these measures were clearly major moves in the direction of dealing with offenders who do reach the Courts in a 'justice' rather than a 'welfare' manner. One of the early impacts of the Act has been to cause a decrease in the use of detention centres and a greater use of the former borstal, now youth custody provision.

Tutt and Giller (1985) analysed some of the outcomes of the 1982 Act. They observed that the 'charge and control provision' (which led many to expect an upsurge in residential care placements) has been virtually unused, that custodial sentencing has increased and concluded that by concentrating greater attention at the polar extremes of the system, diversion on the one hand and custody on the other, the redevelopment of middle range alternatives, typified by intermediate treatment and supervised activities, was proving problematic. In this analysis the Community Homes with Education had clearly been dismissed from having any part in the middle ground, although it was recognised that:

> *...intentions to create more 'law and order' have led to greater emphasis on diversion, intentions to strengthen supervision have led to a decline in it use and restrictions on the use of custody have lead to more young people receiving custodial sentences.*

There has been a significant change in the sentencing practices of the Courts, particularly in the use of care orders and custodial sentences. In 1973 8% of the sentences imposed were Care Orders and 6% penal disposals. In 1983 Care Orders were 3% of the disposals and custodial sentences 10%. Community Homes with Education have clearly declined in a ranging torrent of conflicting ideas about the most effective ways of dealing with delinquency.

This struggle has also been reflected to some extent in the CHEs themselves with debates about their role and function. All this has happened amid financial constraints on local authorities, which has loomed larger with each year from the mid 1970s onwards. The attempt to turn Approved Schools into Community Homes and incorporate them into the general social services provision for children failed. This was largely because CHEs continued to be seen as a resource primarily for children, who while having complex and often disordered family circumstances, were offending against the law. The benefits of the post 1969 Act developments included greater emphasis on community care and the questioning of the necessity of residential care. The shortcomings have been the confused thinking and policies on the right response to juvenile delinquency. Care Orders, imposed on offenders for welfare reasons, have been seen by some simply as punishment and thus inappropriate. The Children and Young Persons Act 1989, implemented in October 1991, abolished the power of the Court to make a Care Order in respect of a child who has committed an offence. If Care Orders can no longer be imposed and penal measures lack impact this can be perceived by people in the communities in which many of the young offenders live as a lack of concern for either the needs of the children or the problems they cause.

Multiple cautions are open to be viewed as impotence on the part of the police. The time is fast approaching when the only option left to a Court, which decides a child needs a period away from its home environment, is to place him or her in the penal system. This, far from being a progressive state of affairs, seems to be a considerable backward step in the care and control of children and young people who have become delinquents.

Thirteen

Between the Anvil and the Hammer

Had a Minister announced in 1978 that most of the 110 Community Homes with Education operating at that time were to be closed in the course of the next 12 years there would certainly have been serious objections to the abandonment of a service built up, in its various guises, since 1854. This concern would have arisen not simply from feelings of nostalgia or a wish to prolong a system with some authoritarian basis, though for some these would have been a factor. Primarily, however, the anxiety would presumably have been about the loss of a service considered to be clearly needed by some children in a society with significant levels of juvenile crime and family neglect. In fact no such announcement was made then or thereafter because there was no plan to shut down the CHE system. Indeed the closures had taken place in such a piecemeal fashion that, until recent years, there had been no general awareness, even among many of the professional workers associated directly with the Homes, that the system as a whole had been disintegrating.

One of the few practitioners to understand what was happening was John Burns, the Principle of Kingswood Community Home with Education, Bristol and President of the Community Homes Association between 1976-77. He told the Association conference in 1976 that the CHEs were then in the position of being between the hammer and the anvil, with central government answering pleas for assistance by saying the problem was to be solved at local level and the local authorities being deprived of the resources needed to sustain CHEs (Burns, 1977). The Government Department directly concerned with overseeing the CHE system, the Department of Health and Social Security, seemed evasive and uncertain about what was happening to the CHEs. This was well illustrated in 1986 in a DHSS response to an enquiry about closures by the National Union of Teachers:

Shortly before and during the period in question changes in the provision of community homes have taken place. As local authorities moved from planning provision on a regional basis towards planning their own provision to meet the needs of children in care it has become less easy to classify particular community homes as CHEs. While a number of the former approved schools, which originally were referred to as CHEs, have closed, their functions have been taken over by other community homes having more than one role.

Whilst there was naturally some accuracy in this statement there was also some avoidance of the basic issue. A large number of CHEs had definitely ceased to function and had, in the process, to inform the DHSS when this happened. When similar enquiries to the DHSS had been made by the author in 1984 about the number of closures, no reply was received. (A response to the question tabled in Parliament by Guy Barnett was answered in positive terms, stating that on 31 March 1986 there were some 89 CHEs in existence; this calculation was based on the use of the term CHE in its broad definition, as noted in the letter to the NUT above.)

Further difficulties in obtaining relevant data were met when local authorities were questioned about closures in a survey of 40 authorities by the author in 1984. Although 29 replied with some information none of the information was given in any great depth. This was due, no doubt, partly to the pace of events in local authorities which had been such that a closure had been but a passing occurrence quickly forgotten once completed.

A more detailed set of questions was presented to 11 local authority and voluntary agency providers of 21 CHEs. Responses were received (in 1986) from agencies responsible for 16 CHEs. Supplementary information about a number of specific closures was also obtained from Maurice Logan-Salton in 1987. (Logan-Salton was Chair of the Criminal Justice Committee of the Conservative Monday Club and a local authority social worker. He had written frequent letters of protest at closures to local and national newspapers and elicited correspondence from many in authority.) By these means it has been possible to obtain a clear indication of the scale of the closures and the outcome of such events, both for those CHEs involved in closure and for the Community Homes with Education system in general.

Most of the closures were effected with the minimum of fuss or resistance. The Association of Community Homes seemed unable to do anything to stem the tide. This was partly due to the loss of the cohesion that the Approved Schools had experienced when they lost their status as a completely separate system under the auspices of the Home Office. It was also, in part, the result of the Heads of the ex Approved Schools trying to hold on to their former special status. Because of this they spent a considerable time arguing about whether they should merge with the ordinary staffs association (see, for example, correspondence in the *Community Schools Gazette*, March 1975).

It was not until mid 1975 that the Association for the Heads and Matrons and that for the Staff came together to form one Association, the Community Home Schools Association. By that time the dye was cast. The new Association never really established any generally agreed policy on closures. Indeed they appeared, in their Executive Council, to be preoccupied with negotiations to ensure that their salaries did not become assimilated into the lower pay structures of the mainstream community home system rather than with the closure issue. In their salary contention they were successful. They also succeeded, in 1980, in securing for staff paid on Joint Negotiating Committee scales an increase in annual leave from eight weeks to fourteen weeks. All of these achievements, of course, escalated staff costs, the major element of expenditure in any CHE budget.

The teacher/care staff difficulties continued to be an issue as a result of separate pay and conditions of service arrangements. With the increased emphasis on care many of the teaching and senior staff felt their status to be undermined. These divisions proved a serious distraction from the basic issue of survival.

For many, the prospects of closure seemed highly remote, a view expressed by David Evans, the President of the Association of Community Home Schools (Evans, 1975):

> *So here I am apparently trying to talk us all out of a job. I doubt if anyone here would be less than delighted if we could close*

down all our establishments tomorrow. But the simple fact is that we cannot, nor are we ever likely to. To do so would depend upon the public at large being prepared to tolerate and accept responsibility for a disruptive element in their midst.

While the staff of the CHEs and their professional association remained preoccupied with conditions of service issues, growing financial constraints and increasing advocacy of community based methods for dealing with delinquent children started gradually to have an impact, and local authorities and voluntary agencies began to close their CHEs.

The year that marked the beginning of the trend was 1978, thereafter the closures occurred yearly with increased pace. By 1990 there had been 79 closures and more were planned (see Appendix D for a list of the CHEs closed between 1978 and 1990). There has been a decimation of the network of CHEs, all of which, with the exception of three, were in existence prior to the 1969 Act, although a few then operated under different names, including Crouchfield (formerly Herts Training) and Polebrook House (Desford). As a result only 24 CHEs (see Appendix E) remained open in 1990 and at least five of these have since closed or are due to close shortly.

A breakdown of the data on closures, as summarised in Table 13, indicate a number of clear trends. It is clear that the Voluntary (Assisted Status) CHEs have been slightly more prone to closure than the local authority and/or controlled status establishments. The number of local authorities managing CHEs fell from 51 in 1978 to 14 in 1990 and the number of voluntary agencies fell from 15 to 4.

This trend shows that it has become increasingly the exception for local authorities or voluntary child care agencies to manage a CHE rather than, as was the case less than a decade ago, the norm. Other factors that emerge from the figures are that those CHEs which moved to becoming co-educational closed more rapidly than the single sex CHEs. This could be an indication that developing a mixed CHE was a final attempt at survival or that the CHEs functioned better as single sex establishments. Boys' CHEs have closed less rapidly than the girls.

In 1985 a short questionnaire (see Appendix F) was sent by the author to 40 local authorities and voluntary agencies known to provide CHEs, seeking information about closures

Table 13
Number of Community Homes with Education in 1978 and 1990

CHEs	1978	1990
Local Auth	88	19
Vol Org	22	5
Boys	69	18
Girls	27	6
Mixed	14	0
Total	110	24

from 1974 onwards. Respondents were asked to give closure dates, reasons for closure, the impact on the children resident in the CHE, the outcome for staff and the subsequent use made of the building. Twenty-three local authorities and six voluntary agencies responded with data about 34 CHE closures which represented 51.5% of the total closures up to 1985. This is, therefore, a significant source of data on the closure trends.

All but seven of the 34 CHEs were owned or controlled by local authorities. The local authorities represented were from all Regions, except Wales, and collectively show a national move away from the use of CHE provision. Some authorities which had maintained a high number of CHEs were shown to have gradually divested themselves of them, for example Hertfordshire and Avon, while others tried to rationalise their resources by merging two or more into one establishment, for example in Cheshire. Only one of the voluntary agencies in the survey, National Children's Home, showed a continuing commitment to residential care and education, by changing the use of its CHEs to that of special school. The Roman Catholic CHEs indicated that their powerful and persistent case for a specialist denominational provision in the days of the Approved School service had collapsed. This was probably because with regionally, as opposed to nationally, based services the arguments were more difficult to sustain and also because of a general disregard of religious affiliation in the placement practices of local authorities.

The consequences of closure for staff of CHEs were that the vast majority were redeployed to other posts within Local Authorities. These appointments, were usually to other child care establishments in social services or education departments. Sometimes, by agreement, the posts were in areas of work distinctly different from previous employment, such as an adviser on child care or work in services for the elderly. Only one voluntary agency in the survey, the Hexham and Newcastle Rescue Society, is recorded as requiring all of its staff to take redundancy or early retirement. The fact that the vast majority of the staff of CHEs were able to be offered other work, voluntary redundancy or early retirement eased the closure process considerably. Had the CHEs been, like their predecessors the Approved Schools, part of a separate national network of services this would not have been possible to the same extent.

Most respondents in the survey looked deeper into the reasons for closure beyond attributing it to 'falling numbers', although five, did give this as their answer.

Some replies undoubtedly masked issues that sometimes lay behind the official explanations for closure such as the political in fighting, the need to balance budgets, and the relief, in some instances, at laying down the burden of running large and complex resources. The majority of replies (17) gave change in child care policies as the main reason for closure. Some pointed to the drop in the child in care population of the providing authority (Essex) and others for example, Devon, to the fact that the providing authority did not need the resource. A few replies pointed out that what was being offered was a regional resource and that user authorities were now choosing not to send their children to the CHE (e.g. St Benedict's and Kneesworth). A few (3) gave the merger of child care resources within the local authority as the reason for closure. One (National Children's Home) stated that 'closure' was in reality a change of use to a special school. These responses underline the fact that most CHEs were part of a regional service so that even if the provider wished to continue, once demand from some parts of the region dropped the CHE became vulnerable to closure. The result has increasingly been that those CHEs which survive have become national resources.

To use 'falling numbers' or 'lack of demand' as an explanation for closure, was of course to beg the question: Why did numbers fall? The answer, as most have acknowledged, was because of a change of policy in the use of residential care. With a general loss of confidence in residential care and with economic pressures it has often taken a strong nerve and firm resolution by existing providers to persevere in maintaining their CHEs. Some have shown that they did not have either. Certainly, for voluntary agencies, the risk of persevering with a CHE has been even more daunting and potentially more economically devastating than for a local authority.

The DHSS had, through its Development Group, devoted much time and effort throughout the 1970s and into the early 1980s in an endeavour to ensure that staff, philosophy and buildings adopted a more child centred approach. Many buildings had been structurally modified or added to at considerable expense. It was regrettable that staff were dispersed and buildings disposed of in ways that often seemed to add little to the child care service as a whole or bring any significant financial recompense to that service. The closures were rarely part of a carefully planned child care strategy.

Many of the buildings in which the CHEs operated did not belong to the local authority managing the service. They were often the property of well established trusts and when the CHE closed it was not for the local authority to dispose of or make use of a particular building, since it had to revert back to the trustees. The majority of properties in the survey were 'sold' or 'disposed of' and put to a variety of other uses, unrelated to child care. In all but seven instances the buildings are likely to have been lost as child care facilities for ever. A further survey, however, (Jenkins, 1987) of 12 closures suggested a greater child care use for former CHEs, (8 out of 12 properties being used for this purpose). The dispersal, redundancy or early retirement of the staff of CHE's and the loss of so many buildings to the child care service over such a short period, and with only limited alternative child care developments suggests a considerable squandering of a large part of the inheritance of the specialist residential child service.

Although there continues to be a network of boarding schools for children with special needs, there is little evidence that there has been any planned move, other than in a few instances by voluntary organisations such as the National Children's Home, to make provision for young people, who could have been sent to CHEs, to be accommodated in special schools. From the author's own experience and that of colleagues all the indications are that most special schools exclude children who become persistent offenders. There is, however, limited research into this aspect of special education. *Residential Care*

-*The Research Reviewed* (Wagner, 1988b) suggests that there has been a general decline in special boarding education, except for children deemed as having emotional and behavioural difficulties. The number of children in the special schools rose from 4000 in 1962 to 12,500 in 1983. This does indicate that some children who would have previously been placed in a CHE have been sent to special boarding schools.

Fourteen

Endings

The closure of a Community Home with Education was not a simple affair. Many had been operating for decades and some, in various guises, for over a century. The children and young people had to be told of the impending closure, and this, for some, was yet a further disruption to their troubled lives. Local authorities, who used the facility, had to be informed and case conferences called to decide the future of the remaining children. Staff had to be prepared for redundancy, early retirement or redeployment. This often involved discussions with trade unions and staff associations. The contents of the building and the building itself had to disposed of. The formal procedures, laid down under the Children and Young Persons Act 1969, had to be followed. This included advising the Secretary Of State for Health and Social Security of the decision to close. Below are some accounts of how this process was experienced by a number of individual Community Homes with Education.

In order to obtain the data for the detailed accounts of closures a number of individuals across a range of both voluntary agencies and local authorities were approached. They had either been Heads of CHEs or in senior management positions in agencies which had closed CHEs. Information was also sought from sources suggested by some of the respondents.

Those approached had close association with 21 CHEs and responses were received about the closure of 16 Homes. The author had had first hand experience of the closure of two of the CHEs, Benton Grange in Newcastle-Upon-Tyne and St Peters, Nr. Darlington, and so had a considerable amount of data on their demise. The Head of one CHE, Sydney Jones, had written a detailed contemporaneous account of the closure of his establishment, Polebrook in Leicestershire (Jones, 1985). Background information about closure of the Royal Philanthropic School was obtained. Valerie Jenkins provided data concerning a study she was undertaking about the closure of a CHE in Sheffield. Data was also received from G. Mercier (Crouchfield), G. Gentry (Daneford), M. Wright (Egerton House), and P. Wright (St Hildas), all Heads of these CHEs at the time of their closure. Information about the closure of five CHEs managed by the largest of the Roman Catholic agencies in England, Liverpool Catholic Social Services, was provided by its Director, Bridget Fann. Data on the closure of one of a number of girls' CHEs managed by a Roman Catholic order of nuns, The Good Shepherd Order, was also provided. Finally, some detail of the closure of a CHE managed by the Leeds Catholic Children's Welfare Society was made available. Although only four accounts were sufficiently detailed to allow for a full examination of the events surrounding closure, the remainder give valuable additional insights. (See Appendix G for details of questions put to respondents).

THE CLOSURE OF POLEBROOK HOUSE

Most CHEs closed relatively quietly and recorded little detail about the closure process. Polebrook House is unique in that the Principal at the time of its closure, Sydney Jones, had kept a full record of events. He, his staff and others were, as far as can be ascertained, the only staff group to fight in a sustained manner (albeit unsuccessfully) the closure of their establishment.

Polebrook was opened in 1881 by Leicester City School Board under the provisions of the Industrial Schools Act 1856 and subsequently became an Approved School known as Desford. At its closure, there were places for 50 boys and girls aged from 12 years. It had been provided with secure provision, but this was never used. It also specialised in 'independence training.' The staffing consisted of a Principal, 3 Deputies, 10 teachers, 32 residential care staff and 25 ancillary staff.

Polebrook was a substantial resource, situated in 50 acres of land, with eight separate self-contained living units completed in 1982, a separate teaching block made up of classrooms, with science, woodwork, art and pottery facilities, a horticultural unit, a painting and decorating workshop and general workshops and a sports hall. There were 24 staff houses on the campus and eight single person flats. The whole property was owned by Leicestershire County Council.

Sydney Jones was, at the time, one of the new breed of

Heads who had moved into the old Approved Schools to apply the philosophy of the DHSS, as enunciated in its report *Care and Treatment In a Planned Environment* (DHSS, 1970). Jones wrote a booklet on the events, from which much of the following information was obtained (Jones, 1985). He became Principal of Polebrook in 1973 when there were a 100 boys in residence and the weekly charge was £36 per child. The building was then a large purpose built school block around a central courtyard. The boys were accommodated in four large dormitories and each 'house' group of about 30 boys had one room available for recreation.

A major building programme was set under way in 1977, with the erection of four purpose built units being completed in 1979. Against the wishes of the Principal an eight place secure unit was completed in 1982. More residential care staff were employed and, by 1983, most of the residents (both boys and girls) came from within 10 miles of Polebrook. Individual care programmes were devised for all residents.

The philosophy was child centred but recognised the need for structure and direction. Polebrook enjoyed the support of the Director of Social Services and of the officers who had direct management responsibility for the school. Some social workers in the department were known, however, to have considered the regime too harsh and to have believed that the resources could be used more effectively elsewhere.

The idea of closure, however, seemed remote. In 1983, £1.6m was spent on redevelopment of Polebrook, including a grant of £175,000 from the DHSS for the secure unit. The closure proposals, when they came, seemed to have much to do with the political in-fighting on the County Council. Up until 1983 Leicestershire had been controlled for many years by the Conservatives. After the local elections of 1981 they lost overall control of the Council and needed to share power with the Liberals.

The focus for hostility to Polebrook was the secure unit. The Labour Group put down a motion not to open the unit. This was defeated in May 1982.

New staff were appointed to manage the secure unit and were due to start work on 1 August 1982. However in mid-June there was a change of political alignment on the Council. The Liberals decided to withdraw their support for the Conservatives and so the Labour group took charge of all

Chairs of the various Committees. One of the first decisions of the newly formed Social Services Committee was to stop the opening of the new secure unit. The local media made much of the issue and Jones gave his support publicly to the unit opening, as he considered that plans were now too far advanced to be changed. This incurred the displeasure of the ruling party. The Chairman and Vice Chairman (who was a social worker from a neighbouring authority) of the Social Services Committee came to placate the staff who sought assurances that there was no plan to close the whole CHE. Although this assurance was given staff remained sceptical.

A working party was then set up to examine the child care policy of the authority. The working party never visited Polebrook. In November 1983 the entire staff group, were gathered together and told that the working party had considered two options in respect of Polebrook, one a reduction in numbers, the other total closure. It had been decided to accept the closure recommendation. The argument for this was that the money saved would be used to provide extra staff in the mainstream community homes. Although the staff were told that they would be re-deployed and that their salaries would be protected, they were extremely distressed at the news and a number resolved to fight the plan.

The Principal immediately informed the young people in care of the news and tried to reassure them about their futures. The atmosphere was one of sadness, anxiety and anger. The staff formed an action committee to prepare to persuade Councillors not to vote for the recommendation when the Social Services Committee met on 21 December 1983. The staff group produced a professional working broadsheet with which to argue their case.

The Principal wrote personally to every Committee member and also invited each of them to visit the CHE. No Labour or Liberal Councillor visited, though a number of Conservatives did and promised support. The Liberal Group agreed to meet a small staff group at County Hall. The staff visited their own County Councillors and the local Member of Parliament. The newspapers led an outcry against the closure when they discovered the news. The Lord Lieutenant of the County, who was also President of the Magistrates Association, wrote to the Social Services Committee asking them not to close Polebrook, as did the Chairman of two local benches.

Jones said he never thought the resistance to closure would succeed but on principle believed it to be a wrong decision that had to be challenged. The vote to close was narrowly carried in Committee in December but the Conservatives required that the decisions should come before the full Council for ratification. This happened in January 1984.

There were 70 full time equivalent posts in Polebrook. All staff were interviewed by senior staff from the social services department to find out their preferences for the future. Some of the ancillary staff took early retirement and the remainder were redeployed. Teaching staff were also redeployed, though were allowed to remain at the CHE until its closure. The care staff were redeployed, with many placed in other posts well before the closure. The speed at which this was done led the Principal to ask for the process to be suspended for fear that all of the care staff would be moved before the young people had been placed. Some staff made it clear they wished to stay until all the youngsters had been properly resettled. Even though the redeployment terms were generous financially, many staff were distressed for some time and many kept in close touch with each other and with the Principal after the closure.

At the time of the announcement of closure there were 36 young people at Polebrook. This number was low because there was a national industrial dispute involving the care staff during which time admissions had been suspended. Five children were awaiting admission. The industrial action did not strengthen the case for retaining Polebrook.

Of the 36 young people 19 were likely to have been discharged in the succeeding months in the natural course of events. In January and February 1984 care conferences were held on every child, at which representatives from the Education Department and the Intermediate Treatment services were present. Nine children were placed in their own homes speedily, with facilities to return to the home on a day basis to complete CSE studies.

After a follow up of the progress of the young people two years after they were discharged (see Table 14), Jones observed that 'some of the young people's later careers may well have been much the same if they had not left Polebrook prematurely but many of those who ended up in custody or experienced homelessness would have returned to Polebrook and gone through our independence programme and would have been

Table14
Placement of Children after Closure of Polebrook House in 1984

Subsequent Placement	Number
Residential Care	9
Custody	8
Home & Offending	2
Home & Pregnant	3
Home & Progressing	10
Unknown	3
Total	35

Data from Jones, 1985

offered long term support' (Jones, 1985). He also noted that despite the expansion of the Intermediate Treatment service none of the discharged young people was offered a place on the programme because they did not meet the criteria.

Very few of the young people returned to mainstream education and only the one child who was later transferred to another CHE took the CSE examinations. Thus, despite the wish of the Committee that no child would suffer the fact is that most did so' according to Jones' records.

Polebrook House formally closed on 13 July 1984. Jones remains convinced that the closure was a major mistake and that 'many young people were denied the chance of experiencing what we offered'. He also noted that 4,989 young people had been catered for in the 103 years of Polebrook/Desford's existence.

A letter from the Chairman of Leicester City Juvenile Court Panel, Alan Clayton, (19 December 1983) to the Members of the Social Services Committee raised some significant points. He believed there would always be a few children who will not respond, 'to other forms of treatment', and that it was essential that these should be properly contained in a firm environment with an educational facility. Only the Social Services Department were in a position to provide this. Clayton considered that the attitudes in schools were such that difficult children were frequently suspended and to all intents and purposes abandoned by the system, although he understood the difficulties presented to teachers by disruptive children. He concluded that Polebrook House was the only possible alternative to a custodial containment for many young people and was amazed by reports of the proposed closure.

The editorial of the *Leicester Mercury* on 4 December 1983, put the closure down to the 'Leicestershire socialists...fixation with intermediate treatment'. Yet despite the support of the local Conservative Member of Parliament Adam Butler, Central Government remained unmoved. In a letter to Norman Fowler, Secretary of State for Health and Social Security on 12 January 1984, Adam Butler suggested that it would appear that there had been 'a failure to act responsibly' on the part of the Social Services Committee. He went on to say 'If you have powers to call it in, I would have thought there was a strong case for an Inquiry'.

The response he received from Mr Fowler's Under Secretary, Tony Newton MP, on 4 March 1984, all but confirmed that Mr Fowler believed the Socialists in Leicestershire to be right and the Conservatives wrong. He began by stating that it was 'not a matter in which the Secretary of State feels able to intervene' and then went on to point out that:

> *Local authorities have been encouraged to look critically at their policies for children in care with particular reference to making more efficient use of the residential sector. An important factor in such a review is that the rationalisation of under-used residential provision can often release considerable resources for application in other services.*

What did concern Mr Newton was the future of the secure unit 'since its construction was funded by way of 100% capital grant from the Department'.

A further response to Adam Butler, from John Patten MP, another Under Secretary of State with the DHSS, on 10 May 1984, specifically applauded Leicestershire's policies and added that:

> *The Department will be monitoring Leicestershire's strategy closely, especially as it contains some interesting and innovative features.*

The account of the closure of Polebrook by Jones provided a unique and valuable insight into the closure of a CHE. By resisting the closure in the manner which he and his staff did, they elicited explicit statements that reflected many of the attitudes and issues that led to the decline of the CHEs.

Polebrook was closed by a Labour controlled Council, with active assistance from the Liberals and with a Vice Chairman of Social Services Committee who was a field social worker in a neighbouring local authority. Their reasons for closure were primarily ideological - their belief that residential care was an unnecessary and inefficient infringement on the lives of young people. The response of the Magistracy and local Conservatives was to challenge this argument. They denied the claim that young people could not benefit from a CHE placement and asserted that society needed such a facility for some youngsters. This clearly had been the belief of the previous Council who had invested over a million pounds in upgrading the building. When the opponents of closure turned to a Central Government, run by their own Party, they found that far from receiving support they were told that the Council's decision to close Polebrook made economic sense.

This closure highlights the rapid pace of the change in policy for young offenders. The results, in this instance, were that some of the young people in residence suffered further disruption in their already chaotic lives, that some staff talents were lost to the child care profession and that a valuable building in which much money and effort had been invested was lost to child care. All this occurred before alternative measures were properly established and found to be effective.

The closure also exposed the role of mainstream education in this whole process. A letter from the Chairman of the Leicester City Juvenile Panel claimed that 'only the Social Services Department' were in a position to make provision for residential care and education of disturbed and delinquent children and that many of these children have 'been abandoned' by schools. He also claimed that many school teachers are powerless to deal with disruptive children. It would seem right to question why *only* the social services department could provide a response to the problem when it is one that is also of concern for the education departments. Even the Warnock Committee, simply accepted that CHEs were the province of the Social Services Departments, whilst arguing that teachers should be 'in the service of the local educational authorities' (Warnock, 1978). (This issue is explored further below.) In none of the accounts of closure obtained was there any reference to the local Education Department being consulted about the closure, or expressing any interest. This underlines the compartment approach by both local and central government to the issues of child care, education and juvenile delinquency.

THE CLOSURE OF ST PETERS

The second account concerns St Peters which was one of the two CHEs managed by the Hexham and Newcastle Diocesan Rescue Society, now Catholic Care North East, with whom the author at present holds a senior management position. The author was in post at the time of closure. The information, therefore, is known in considerable detail from first hand experience and is supported by a number of documents and letters.

St Peters was situated in a rural area just outside the village of Gainford in County Durham, and offered places for 60 boys aged from 11 years. It had opened in 1900 as a Roman Catholic institution for homeless children, and became an Approved School in 1942. St Peters was set in 32 acres of land beside the River Tees. The building itself was large, sprawling and barrack-like in appearance. It had a modern classroom block, a gymnasium and sports fields. There were staff flats, bungalows for the Principal and Deputy Principal and a staff house, all on the campus, and staff housing in close proximity.

At the time of closure in 1984, the staffing consisted of the Principal, Deputy Principal, Head of Education, Training Officer, 4 Housewardens, 22 residential care staff, 7 teachers, maintenance men, gardener, 2 administration staff, and cooking and domestic staff - some 56 staff in total. The CHE was owned and managed by the Catholic social work agency for the diocese in which St Peters was located and had assisted status with Cleveland County Council.

The closure of St Peters should be seen in the context of concern in Regional Planning Area No. 1, from 1980 onwards, about the number of CHE places required in the Region. In 1981 the Regional Planning Committee had created a working group of Senior Officers from various Authorities in the Region to review CHEs with special reference to the overprovision of places. This group reported back to the Committee that there were 140 boys places surplus to requirements, out of an existing total of 540. The 150 girls places were considered necessary. Critical remarks were made about two CHEs, the Castle School Stanhope and St Peters, and it was recommended that these should be closed.

Cleveland County Council who managed The Castle School and 'assisted' St Peters were quite happy with this recommendation, but the Hexham and Newcastle Rescue Society strenuously defended the practice at St Peters and the need for the CHE to continue. In the event, the Regional Planning Committee did not pursue the recommendations that facilities should be closed as a result of the assessment of their practice and resources. Instead they left it to individual local authorities to make suggestions as to how to bring about the reduction in numbers. As a result, St Peters was not closed at this time. In its place Newcastle upon Tyne sought agreement to its proposal to close Axwell Park's CHE at Blaydon. The Castle CHE did, however, close in 1982.

The Region attempted to create a clearer and more specialist structure for its CHE provision and a further working group was given the task of developing these proposals. In 1982 it produced a review of services for difficult children and their families, in which it was recommended that there be a concerted attempt to integrate the CHE system into the total provision for children and families. This report laid down an ambitious programme to bring together both local and regional services and was accepted in principle by the Regional Planning Committee in 1982.

Events were, however, overtaking this belated attempt at integration. Individual local authorities began making their own decisions about closures. Although they still formally sought the approval of the Regional Planning Committee to proceed with their plans (and also Regional funding to cover the costs of closure) there was little likelihood that these proposals would be rejected. This was because of the general agreement that such closures would ultimately save all the participant authorities expenditure, and because no one wanted to deny that, in practice, each authority retained the right to exercise its powers over its own establishments.

The change in the law in respect of Regional Planning under the terms of the Health and Social Services Adjudication Act, 1983 led the local authority Councillors to resolve to end the pooling arrangements on 31 March 1984 and, in the absence of any agreement on an alternative co-operative grouping, the local authorities regional dialogue ceased. It would appear that once finance was removed from the agenda there was little incentive left for the self sufficient local authorities to consult with their less well endowed neighbours.

The prospect of the removal of the financial cushion of the Regional Pooling arrangement had led the Hexham and Newcastle Rescue Society to write to all local authorities in the Region in October 1983 asking about their projected future use of St Peters. Only the assisting authority, Cleveland, saw any likely use of St Peters, and this for only seven places. In the light of these responses it seemed prudent to close St Peters rather than risk serious losses as a result of low occupancy and additional closure costs. If the Society closed St Peters before the end of March 1984 the constituent authorities in the Region, as they had done with the other closures, would meet the costs of this exercise.

The staff had been kept fully informed of these possibilities as soon as they became apparent in October 1983. A further meeting was called in November 1983 to advise staff that the consultation with local authorities had shown that they foresaw no future need for St Peters and that it was to be closed on 31 March 1984. At the time of the announcement there were 40 boys in the CHE. Ironically, because of an industrial dispute amongst local authorities and residential workers, a further 12 boys were admitted on a short term basis up to the period December 1983 when all further admissions were then refused. The boys were all told of the closure plan on the same day as the staff and generally were upset and unsettled by the prospect.

Of the 52 boys discharged from the date of the closure announcement 20 or so (including some of the short-term placements) would, in any event, have returned home over that period; for the remaining 32 boys the closure meant yet a further disruption in their lives. Case conferences were called on every boy to make the best arrangements possible (see Table 15). Twenty-five boys were discharged by Christmas 1983, six by the end of January 1984 and eight by the end of February. The last boy left St Peters on 28 March 1984.

When the closure plans were announced to St Peters staff there were 56 full and part time staff in post. The longest serving member of staff had been in post for 33 years. Eight of the teachers and care staff had worked at the CHE for eight or more years. Redundancy payments, in line with those made when other CHEs in the Region closed, came to just over

Table 15
Placement on Closure of St Peters in 1984

Placement	Number
Home on Trial	34
Children's Home	7
Youth Custody	2
Special School	2
Remand Centre	1
Special Clinic	1
Other CHE	5
Total	52

£70,000. Six of the staff took early retirement. Many staff had difficulty in finding other suitable employment.

The managers of St Peters accepted that the Rescue Society had genuinely explored the future viability of the CHE and that they had reluctantly made the only prudent decision. There was some belated outcry from a few members of the public but no concerted effort was made that offered any realistic alternative to closure.

St Peters was put on the open market by the owners, the Roman Catholic Diocese of Hexham and Newcastle. The building was sold in November/December 1984 to a local consortium. Over £40,000 had had to be spent on wages, heating, rates up to the time of its sale. The building and the land were sold for £130,000. The buyers subsequently sold some of the dwellings and converted one wing into a nursing home for the elderly. The need to repay the DHSS for improvement grants made by the DHSS or Home Office in earlier years added still further to the financial burden for a small voluntary agency after offering a service to the State for so many years.

THE CLOSURE OF BENTON GRANGE

The second CHE managed by the Hexham and Newcastle Diocean Rescue Society was Benton Grange. It had been owned and managed by a Roman Catholic Order, The Good Shepherd Sisters, up until 1978. They then leased it for 10 years to the Society. The author was Headmaster of this CHE from 1977-1981.

Benton Grange had originally been opened in 1889 by the Good Shepherd Order. It was a large solid structure with all its living and educational facilities in the one building. It had also a small secure unit for three girls. Located in an urban area, the town centre of Newcastle was 15 minutes distance on public transport. Originally it offered places for 44 girls but this was reduced to 40 in 1978, 34 in 1983 and 22 in 1984. The reductions were an attempt to retain the CHE with a smaller number of girls and staff but, ultimately, the low number was not viable.

The staffing consisted of a Head, 2 Deputies, a Head of Education plus 6 teachers, 22 care staff, a Bursar and an assistant Bursar, half time nurse, a secretary, two maintenance staff and a cook and domestic staff. The cost per week at the time of closure (1984) was £377 per child per week.

Considerable effort had been made by the managing agency to retain Benton Grange as a CHE. In 1983 a managers' working party and a staff working party had been appointed to explore ways of ensuring its future. In August 1983 a 17 point plan for the future development of Benton Grange was presented, following the exploration of various options. Amongst those explored had been the development of the CHE into a special school for girls. The Secretary of the Northern Council of Educational Committees had responded to this idea by stating that 'LEA (Local Education Authority) provision in the Region of the Northern Council of Educational Committees, with particular reference to provisions for disturbed children in need of special education, was likely to be adequate for the near future'. The option of special residential education was not therefore pursued.

There was also little scope for any integration with Newcastle upon Tyne City Education provision. Some way of serving the Catholic network of 22 secondary schools in the Diocese was also explored. The difficulty was that, although a number of Heads of Catholic schools expressed interest in the idea of referring difficult girls to Benton Grange, there was no system for doing this since the schools were located in eight different local authority areas which, on the evidence of the Northern Council, could see no need for additional provision.

The model of provision offered by Barnardos at Druids Heath CHE in the Midlands was also explored. This approach involved a small network of residential facilities in the community and a main base, used primarily as an education unit and as a family support provision. Support for this proposal was not forthcoming from the local authorities.

Amongst the other points made in the August 1983 Report were the following:

- Authority should be sought to use the Intensive Care unit as a short term authorised Secure Unit for up to four girls.
- A member of staff should be appointed as a Family Liaison Officer.
- The Rescue Society should become responsible for recruiting families and placing   girls in short or long term family placements, where appropriate.
- A separately charged independence unit for eight girls or young women, with or without children, should be developed in the current Hostel Unit.
- The CHE should be known as Benton Grange Community Home and Resource Centre.

Although the proposals were accepted by the Managers and the Staff they never came to fruition. There was little enthusiasm from local authorities for the ideas and reluctance by some staff to become part of a more complex resource.

With the collapse of the Regional Planning Committee and the ending of the Regional Pooling arrangements, the future funding of Benton Grange would depend entirely on fees from referrals. However as the number of girls places provided in CHEs in the Region as at 1 April 1984 was likely to fall from 142, with the closure of one girls' CHE, the probable closure of a second and the conversion of the third into a co-educational CHE, the anticipated eventual number of girls places available in the Region would be only 41. Although only four local authorities, one of whom was out of the Region, took up a proposal to buy in a number of places at Benton Grange (10 places in all), it was nevertheless decided at the end of 1983, despite the demise of the Region, to proceed with offering 22 residential and six day places at Benton Grange.

When, by early May 1984, the number of residents dropped to 16, with the prospect of some discharges at the end of the summer term and virtually no new referrals, it was finally decided that there was no option left other than closure. In a written statement to all staff at Benton Grange on 9 May 1984 the Administrator of The Rescue Society, Dennis Tindall, advised them that he had decided, after consultation with the Managers, the assisting local authority (Newcastle), and with the knowledge and agreement of the Good Shepherd Order, to announce that Benton Grange would cease to be a CHE with effect from 31 August 1984.

The staff were not particularly surprised by the announcement of the closure. Many had become weary of the worry and uncertainty about the future viability of the CHE and accepted the announcement with some relief. The few girls who would have remained in the CHE had it not been closing were distressed when they heard the news. Case conferences were soon arranged and all were discharged by the end of July 1984.

Benton Grange closed with a running cost deficit of £70,653 and staff redundancy payments of £39,653 and £12,000 in supplementary payments under the superannuation scheme. With central government refunds of £15,000 on the redundancy payments, the Society was left with a deficit of £105,000. All Local Authorities in the Region were asked to assist in clearing this debt on the basis that they had been the main beneficiaries of the use of Benton Grange. Four of the nine authorities agreed to make a contribution totalling £29,000. The Society was therefore left with a debt of £76,000.

The Good Shepherd Order agreed to the Society running Benton Grange as student accommodation for two years. With some minor building modification, 50 students took up residence in mid September 1984. This arrangement was to allow the Society to explore other possible uses for the CHE. In 1986 the Order decided to sell the whole property, including the adjoining convent. The building stood empty and unused until, in October 1987, it was demolished. There is now an housing estate of executive style properties on the site.

There is now only one CHE in the former Region 1 that offers a limited number of places for girls. Other than some additional emphasis on intermediate treatment and foster care there is little evidence of any adequate substitute provision for girls in the Region. Given that the majority of girls in CHEs were not offenders, the loss of so much CHE provision will have a limited immediate impact on society. The main reasons for placement had been the serious emotional instability of the girls and the 'moral danger' to which they were exposed. The experience of the author when Head of Benton Grange (1977-

1981) of the depth and range of disturbance of the girls then in residence suggests that many girls with similar problems and needs must now be left in the community with very limited support.

The closure of both St Peters and Benton Grange, illustrate how a voluntary society was forced to relinquish work with disturbed and delinquent young people because of financial pressures and the change of policy of local authorities in respect of the use of residential care. With a substantial financial loss it has been difficult for the Society to develop other community based alternatives.

THE ROYAL PHILANTHROPIC

The Royal Philanthropic of Redhill, Surrey, the longest established CHE, finally closed in 1988. Maurice Logan-Salton elicited correspondence and other data that chronicled the last years of the CHE. This included letters from the Director of Social Services for the controlling Local Authority (the London Borough of Wandsworth), the Parliamentary Under Secretary of State for Health, Edwina Currie, MP, the Principal of the Royal Philanthropic, Walter Campling, Lord Silkin of Dulwich and George Gardiner, MP.

Campling, in a letter of 7 July 1986, gave a cogent account of how events developed at the Royal Philanthropic. When the former Approved School and Classifying School became a CHE in 1973 the trustees had opted for controlled status with the London Borough of Wandsworth. At the time of the change of status, the campus consisted of a CHE for 60 children, a Regional Assessment Centre for 52 children and a Secure Unit for 30 children. All the provision was for boys only. The CHE and the Assessment Centre were closed in 1982 and the Secure Unit in 1983. In place of these facilities a much smaller service, consisting of 20 places for remand and assessment, 12 long stay places and 8 secure places, was offered.

These facilities had been much in demand during the period from 1 January 1983 to 7 July 1986. During that time some 460 boys had been admitted for varying lengths of stay. (Campling stated in a letter of 3 September 1986 that the Secure Unit in particular remained in great demand and that on one day in August 1986 he received no fewer than 17 enquiries for places.)

The Royal Philanthropic had, in fact, begun selling off the large campus once it ceased to be fully operational in 1982/83. The CHE site with workshops, classrooms and staff housing was sold to a developer in 1984. Subsequently, planning permission was granted for the erection of an 'Old People's Village'. The adjoining farm, which had always been a thriving part of the establishment was sold as a going enterprise. The Society has given as its reason for deciding to sell the property a wish to realise the assets tied up in the site and to apply them to other more modern methods of social work intervention in young people's lives.

Logan-Salton's correspondence with Norman Fowler, the Secretary of State for Health and Social Security in August 1986 tells of a somewhat belated attempt to stir up opposition to the closure, in view of the facts given above. It is clear that he was unaware that the closure was so advanced. Nonetheless a number of senior politicians were roused into responding to the issues raised, given that there remained a significant remnant of the Royal Philanthropic. Thus Lord Silkin of Dulwich QC in his letter to The Home Secretary, on 22 September 1986 stated that he shared Logan-Salton's concern that, with the closure of such places as the Royal Philanthropic, there would be a reduction in the number of alternative to custody places for young offenders. He also commented that 'no doubt you and Norman Fowler, have consulted together to make good these gaps.' In her reply (8 October 1986) to Logan-Salton, the Under Secretary of State, Mrs Currie, observed that 'Closure of a number of community homes is, I would suggest, to be expected'.

In a letter received from George Gardiner MP (5 September 1986) it was stated that the Philanthropic Society was not planning to close the CHE. 'All it has said is that in 2-3 years time it will cease to provide free-of-charge premises. If the authorities wish to continue the CHE then they can seek to buy or rent the existing premises, and the Society will consider proposals on their merits'. A subtle point, since it would be unlikely that the amount of cash expected for this type of transaction would be available to Wandsworth Council.

Campling and his staff were clearly unhappy with the Society withdrawing from the arrangements with Wandsworth. He commented:

The Royal Philanthropic Society was founded in 1788 and pioneered social work with delinquent children. Its innovative work paved the way for much of the eventual legisla~~tion~~ introduced during two centuries to ensure that children who offend are dealt with outside the mainstream provision for adult offenders. It does now seem ironical that their present action will almost inevitably result in more children entering the penal system that would otherwise be the case.

This may have been a harsh judgement on the Philanthropic Society since it was largely the lack of referrals by local authorities in earlier years that had greatly reduced the work on the campus and made it less viable.

What must be regrettable is that the Society plans to withdraw from being involved in any residential provision offering training and education. The new Director of The Society, Donald Coleman, has stated that instead it is intended to develop accommodation for young people who have been in care; a good and necessary work but not wholly in line with its previous history of work with young offenders. The society finally closed the remaining provision at Redhill in June 1988.

DATA ON 12 OTHER CLOSURES

The closure of the Royal Philanthropic was the result of a number of factors many of which were also applicable to other closures studied. The most frequent was finance and the best use of resources, as in the closures of St Hildas, Gosforth, Springhead Park, Sheffield, Danesbury, Hertfordshire and St Camillus, Tadcaster. At St Hildas there was clear evidence that the controlling local authority, Newcastle upon Tyne, decided to use the closure to help balance its social services budget and to improve some of its other child care services. In a financial year, £230,000 was saved.

Of this £100,000 was allocated to improve staffing ratios in children's homes and to improve resources at the observation and assessment centre. The balance was deducted from social services expenditure. (Peter Wright, 1985, pers. comm.). At Crouchfield and Danesbury (Hertfordshire), considerable savings were made in social services budgets as the result of the closures. The figure given for Danesbury (Gentry, 1986, per. comm.) was £750,000. Some of the monies from the closures were used to develop intermediate treatment programmes. The rest was lost to child care services.

A major aspect of the cost of maintaining Springhead Park, Sheffield, and of many other CHEs, was that of the employment of large numbers of staff. This raised the weekly fees to a level that deterred many local authorities from using the service. In Springhead Park, a CHE for 30 girls, there was a Principal, 2 Deputies, a Head of Education, 3 full-time teachers, 2 Group Leaders and a team of residential social workers, a field social worker, a bursar, 2 office staff, a cook, a handyman, a gardener and domestic staff. It is hardly surprising that at the time of its closure in 1986 the weekly charge was £423 per week per girl. Part of the explanation for the policy of providing a high child/ staff ratio was the belief that change in the child could be best achieved through effective interpersonal relationships.

The high charges could only be sustained in a declining market of referrals where Regional Pooling systems operated, which enabled those CHEs with deficits to be reimbursed. Once this collapsed many CHEs, especially those managed on a voluntary basis, faced financial disaster, as in St Peters, Gainford and Benton Grange.

Another example of this was the closure of St Camillus, Tadcaster. At the time of its demise this was a CHE for 45 boys. It had been managed by a voluntary child care agency, the Leeds Catholic Child Welfare Society. There had been no cost pooling arrangements in this instance and as local authorities attempted to sustain their own facilities rather than send the declining number of referrals to a voluntary agency, this type of CHE quickly became a victim of market forces. It closed in August 1983.

Five other voluntary managed CHEs support the evidence that they were generally more vulnerable to closure in the early years of the decline in the use of CHEs than those managed by local authorities. These were St Georges Freshfield, St Aidens Widnes, Greenfield House, St Helens and St Josephs Marshfield. There was a great deal of anger with the local authorities and the Regional Planning Committee for forcing these closures on the voluntaries. Some creative thinking on the part of the agencies concerned emerged as a result of these closures.

In the case of St Josephs, a CHE managed by the Good Shepherd Order, an arrangement was reached with another voluntary agency, Dr Barnardos. This involved the Sisters of the Good Shepherd becoming responsible for the staffing and day to day management of a CHE, owned by Dr Barnardos, Duncroft, in Staines on a limited contractual basis. As a result of this the Head of St Josephs, nine staff and 20 girls transferred to Duncroft. In the cases of two of the CHEs managed by Liverpool Catholic Social Services, St Georges and Greenfield, considerable foresight and tenacity was shown in changing their status from CHEs registered with the DHSS to schools for children with special needs, registered with the DES. Had a similar course of action been advocated in other instances the special residential services for children might have been substantially improved and a number of CHEs could have been enabled to carry on offering a service to children.

It emerged that the closures could be more complex and painful where a number of separate but interested parties were involved. This was apparent in considering the closure of the Royal Philanthropic, with the Society and the local authority adopting differing standpoints. It was even more complex in the case of Eton Lodge CHE in Liverpool.

This was owned by the Sisters of the Good Shepherd Order and managed by Liverpool Catholic Social Services on their behalf, and had assisted status with Liverpool Social Services. The decision to close Eton Lodge was taken by the Good Shepherd Sisters because they no longer had sufficient nuns to manage the CHE. The local authority, and the managing agency, were not pressing for the CHE to close and were unhappy about the decision but, once it had been made, they decided to accept it. The various reasons and differing circumstances of the closures indicate the general disarray into which the CHE began to fall from the early 1980s onwards.

The closures had a dramatic impact on the lives of many people, primarily the CHE staff and residents. The follow-up enquiries by Jones of Polebrook House indicated how poorly many of their former residents behaved after what was often a premature discharge from residential care. The St Peters data also shows that many children were returned home earlier than would have otherwise been the case. The Springhead Park account drew attention to the increased disturbed behaviour of the girls when they learned of the impending closure.

The fact that Polebrook House staff were the only group to mount a sustained challenge to closure plans indicated the absence of any concerted resistance to the closures. The professional associations did little to resist the changes and there are no records of them aiding any of the CHEs that were closed. The work of the CHEs was not generally known to the public. Many of them had operated with only very limited contact with the community (belying their title) and their going did not arouse much, if any, public interest. The managers of the CHEs did not have the power or the status of their Approved School predecessors and so generally felt unable to resist the closures even where they might wish to do so.

Initially the Regional Planning Committees tried to set the pace for the closures. As they were wary of dictating closure decisions to constituent Local Authorities they flexed their muscles on the voluntary agencies.

Thus, St Josephs in Wiltshire, St Camillus in Leeds, and St Aidens, Lancs, each of which were in different Regions and all voluntary agency establishments considered that they had been chosen for closure in preference to a local authority resource. In Region 1 there was evidence of an attempt at an orderly disengagement under the direction of the Regional Planning Committee. This was short lived however and once local authorities began to take unilateral action any thought of Regional needs appeared to have vanished. Once the local authorities started closing their own provision they made no attempt to sustain the remaining voluntary agency CHEs.

Few of those who provided the data for the accounts were satisfied that realistic alternatives for delinquent and emotionally disturbed children were in reality available in the community. It is apparent that the CHE system could only have survived intact where there was a strong belief in its worth. Once that belief collapsed, as it generally did, then there were many arguments readily available to favour its dismantlement. What is perhaps of more concern than the loss of the resources inherited from the past is the general failure to build substantial alternatives for the future.

One of the important changes brought about under the 1969 Children and Young Persons Act was that central government divested itself of direct responsibility for the former Approved Schools - the new CHEs. The only powers retained were to hold a watching brief via the Department of Health and Social Security and a requirement that the Secretary of State had to authorise the CHE coming into being and agree to closures. In the event these powers have been largely formal and have simply endorsed recommendations of lesser bodies, i.e. Regional Planning Committees and local authorities. With government distanced from CHEs, with few powerful advocates and the financial pressures on local authorities their closures have almost been inevitable. The accounts above chronicle individual instances of the effects of these changes in policy on a service that was once seen as a vital element in the management of juvenile delinquency.

Fifteen

The Facts and the Future

The decline of the Community Home with Education system is now not far from being a complete collapse. Its demise will bring to an end an era in which it had been thought both humane and expedient to place some delinquent children in a setting which offered residential care and education.

The CHEs have been closed with surprising ease and over a relatively short period of time. Between 1977 and 1990, 87 CHEs have ceased to operate, leaving just 23 in existence. As a number of these remaining establishments are known to be scheduled for closure it seems reasonable to presume that in a few years time, if the present trend continues, few if any CHEs will remain. Although the closures have been a national phenomenon they have not been carried out in any concerted manner. The pace of events has rather been influenced by local policies and has taken little account of national needs or of the needs of other than the managing agency and some of the neighbouring users. Consideration of national need has not been part of the brief of the providers. It is unfortunate, however, that no one seems to have taken a national viewpoint of the need for CHE provision.

Most of the voluntary child care agencies, except the National Children's Homes and to a limited extent Barnardos and the Liverpool Catholic Social Services have withdrawn from residential care and education in face of declining demand and financial uncertainty. National Children's Homes and Liverpool Catholic Social Services have shown a creative commitment to this provision by seeking dual registration with both DoH and the DES. Local Authorities, for whom such a strategy would have been relatively simple, have not pursued this option.

The CHEs have withered in a climate of confused ideas about juvenile justice, conflicting views about their role and function, hostility to institutional care and general financial restraint. This confused state of affairs bodes ill, not only for the present welfare and future prospects of many young people, but also for the community in general. The CHE system had been at least tangible evidence that society cared both about the offender and his or her victim. The alternative measures, even when applied, have yet to clearly convey this message.

The ideal of creating a system based in local communities has been one of the welcome features of the alternative developments in recent years. It must be questioned, however, whether it has been wise to make such a policy the sole alternative to custodial measures. The ability of the 'community' to cope with a care in the community strategy at a time when there are so many other pressures on it (e.g. unemployment, single parenthood, an ageing population), would seem to be limited.

There has been little detailed thought given to the development of alternatives to residential care and to custody at a national level, and only isolated instances of such thought at a local level. The monies saved from the closures of CHEs have only been partially redirected to developing these measures. Much of the cash has been lost to child care and has been used instead to balance hard pressed local authority budgets.

In spite of alternative methods for dealing with juvenile crime and, from the late 1970s the closure, at an ever increasing rate of the 'ineffective' CHE, crime has continued to rise; recorded crime rose in 1990/91 by 18% on the previous years. The arguments over the effectiveness of the various measures now applied to juvenile delinquents tend to centre on the individuals who have offended. Little account has been taken of the general impact of the new policies on the communities most affected by the activities of young delinquents when, for example, a young offender known to have been apprehended for the third or fourth time for the commission of an offence receives a caution yet again! Nor has the impact on mainstream schools and their staff been considered when known offenders are being 'diverted from court'. There is little evidence that the public at large have been made aware of the new approaches to delinquency or that their views have been taken into account. The result has been that a new system of responding to delinquency has been imposed on an uninformed general public who, especially on large, low income estates, feel they are often living in a situation of near lawlessness.

Those in positions of responsibility in the main statutory provision for children, mainstream education, do not consider that they are equipped to manage young offenders. This was an issue explored by the Warnock Committee in 1978. It was observed that there is a considerable similarity between the educational needs of children in CHEs and those with emotional or behavioural disorders in special schools.

The Report added, somewhat mystifyingly that: 'At the same time we recognise that children who are placed in CHEs require a period of treatment which aims at social readjustment'. Presumably the same is true of children placed in special needs schools. Warnock was on the brink of recommending that CHEs should be integrated into the educational services:

We have therefore considered a proposal for a more fundamental change in the community home system, involving the transfer of the management of CHEs to the education service. We have found merit in this proposal; in particular it would have the advantage of making for a wider and more flexible range of special educational provision for children with emotional and educational disorders.

For reasons, which seem very inadequate, Warnock concluded:

On balance, however, most of us consider such a radical change would be undesirable at the present time, given that the Children and Young Persons Act 1969 has not yet been fully implemented.

The Warnock Report did, however, recommend that, as a first step in improving the quality of educational provision in CHEs and observation and assessment centres, teachers in those establishments should be in the service of local education authorities.

The National Union of Teachers, in its evidence to the House of Commons Select Committee on Social Services for Children in Care (The Short Committee, reporting in 1984) were quite clear that the future of CHEs lies with the education authorities. In their view, despite the need for residential placements for many children, there is a major threat to the continued maintenance of CHEs. They observed that:

In the last 5-10 years there have been a substantial number of CHEs ... that have closed down. This is not as a result of a drop in juvenile crime or delinquency. It is the result, primarily of financial considerations.

The National Union of Teachers affirmed that it believed CHEs should be the responsibility of Local Education Authorities and not social service departments, and there should be much closer links between teachers in CHEs and those in local schools. It held that the facilities in CHEs could be expanded to assist local intermediate treatment courses, and that the education element of CHEs could be developed to cater for day pupils in greater numbers. The National Union of Teachers argued that CHEs should not be just for offenders and drew attention to the many children who just 'roam the streets', and suggested that there are many children in residential special schools who would be better served in CHEs.

The National Union of Teachers supported the views of the Warnock Committee on CHEs and reported that, in evidence to that Committee, it had 'strongly pressed for the transfer of management of CHEs to the education service'.

When the Short Committee finally published its Report in 1984 it dealt with the role of CHEs in one paragraph. The scant attention given to CHEs by the Committee indicated either its lack of awareness of their significance, or a belief that they were irrelevant to modern child care. The comments on CHEs were somewhat confused with a number of other issues. The Report stated:

What is badly needed is a clarification of what they (CHEs) can offer to children, and a review of each and every placement of a child in any CHE to see if they are appropriately placed. It may be that such a review could be undertaken in the context of a more general review of the functions and performance of other local authority boarding schools. At present CHEs still seem uneasily poised between their essentially punitive past and their supposedly therapeutic future.

Four issues were raised in this statement:

- What can CHE's offer children?
- What is the value of a placement for specific children?
- What is the relationship of CHEs to other local authority boarding school provisions?
- Are CHEs poised between a punitive and a therapeutic approach.

These were all interesting and important questions. Regrettably the Short Report did not attempt to answer them nor suggest who should try to do so. With the passing of time and in the light of subsequent events the questions have long since lost their relevance.

When considering the formal education of children in care the Report commented on the concerns expressed by the report of Her Majesty's Inspectorate on CHEs (DES, 1980) and Warnock (1978) about the isolation of teachers in the CHEs from mainstream education. It saw no merit, however, in transferring the management of CHEs, in whole or in part, to educational departments. In making these observations there seemed to be a presumption that the CHE system would continue and the Report therefore only addressed the issue of improving the standard of education. This could probably be achieved, it was suggested, by following the example of some local authorities where the teaching staff were employed by the education authority rather than by social services.

The Committee was probably right in stating that simply transferring the responsibility for CHEs from social service to education departments would not solve either the problems of professional isolation or the future viability of the CHEs. Since central government divested itself of responsibility for the Approved Schools and removed the powers of an independent body, the Magistrates, to decide who should be placed in a residential care and education provision the burden for these decisions has rested with local authorities. It is highly unlikely that another local authority department, education, would willingly take on this responsibility, especially during the current upheaval in the management of mainstream education. The result, therefore, is likely to be, unless there were to be a central government direction indicating a different course of action, that social services will continue to respond to the pressures to reduce expenditure by closing more CHEs. The more closures there are, the more will the remaining few CHEs appear anachronistic. If at the same time, as appears likely, juvenile offending continues at its present level, then a growing minority of older offenders will be placed in penal or secure establishments.

The idea of treating or caring for these young offenders could become foreign to the system and be replaced by a norm of punishment and containment. Indeed the Children Act 1989 specifically removes from the Courts the power to make a care order in respect of a child who has committed an offence. This is based on the principle that a child should not enter care because he or she has committed an offence.

The Criminal Justice Act 1991 establishes separate courts for dealing with offenders, known as Youth Courts. Except for the most serious of crimes, no child or young person under 15 years of age can be made the subject of residential placement as the outcome of a criminal offence. Young offenders aged 15 years and over plus may be sent to a young offender institution, for a minimum of 2 months and a maximum of 12 months if the offender is under 18 years of age. With effect from October 1992 no young people under 17 years of age will be allowed to be remanded in custody. Local authorities will be expected to provide ,or have access to, secure accommodation for young people requiring such containment.

These two major pieces of legalisation are the logical outcome on the belief in the need to separate the response to welfare requirements and to delinquent behaviour. They also fully reflect the philosophy of preventing children and young people becoming subject to legal proceedings unless this proves unavoidable.

For the great majority of children these developments have much to commend them and are the result of enlightened and humane thinking. They fail, however, to take account of the significant minority who are causing considerable concern and distress, both to themselves and others, by their continued delinquent behaviour.

There are some reports in the press that must give rise to serious concern about the lack of effective means for managing young delinquents and for curbing their offending. *The Times*, for example, reported on 9 October 1992 that a boy aged 11 years was sent to secure accommodation following a catalogue of burglaries that included 11 public houses and 17 other properties. It is not suggested that such behaviour is the norm but there is certainly a level of offending in some communities by young people to prompt further thinking about the correct level of response. While the system of cautioning and diversion from court has much to commend it, there remains a distinct danger that over reliance on such system can hide the true scale of the problem of juvenile delinquency.

A strong case remains for an independent body to hear the

facts about an alleged offence and , where confirmed that an incident(s) has occurred, assess its seriousness in terms of the age and understanding of the child, and express formally their views on what action ,if any, needs to be taken. The Scottish Children's Panel system (under the terms of the Social Work (Scotland) Act 1968), seems to be a model worth considering as a means of responding in the way suggested. Justice and welfare can not, in practice, be eliminated from any civilised system for dealing with young offenders. To rely on one or the other will lead to either an unduly harsh or an unacceptably ineffectual response.

Residential care and education should remain an option for a minority of young offenders, both as an opportunity to assist such children in leading a more socially acceptable life and as a reassurance to society at large that where necessary, resources exists both to aid the child and to help preserve good social order. If the residential option is eliminated then a society pushed to desperation in dealing with juvenile delinquency will have little choice other than to take the retrograde step of placing more children in penal or secure institutions.

The CHE system was an honourable attempt to avoid having residential units for offenders alone, both in an attempt to prevent labelling of children and to take pre-emptive action prior to a child being formally charged with an offence instead of waiting until they had become habitual delinquents. The new legislation appears to have accepted that such a goal is unachievable although the low key approach to petty offending does, however, in practice, allow for the opportunity for welfare considerations to be taken into account and a prudent and caring society should take advantage of this.

The cost factors in residential care must be acknowledged. For some children high staffing ratios are needed, both to contain difficult behaviour and to bring about change. For others however, as in the past, it should be possible to create structured units which offer good levels of care and training but which do not require intensive staffing. Costs have to be kept within reasonable bounds if a residential unit with a capable and caring staff with access to material resources is to offer a valuable contribution to the care, education and containment of appropriately placed children. The general aim should be to have a variety of systems and philosophies of residential care and to place a child in the unit that best meets the child's needs.

Such a service might, in the light of the shortcomings of the CHE system, seem to be best overseen by both the education and social services departments but be managed independently possibly by the voluntary sector. Voluntary child care agencies could, if properly resourced, be in a good position to offer such a service. Indeed, the National Children's Home and Liverpool Catholic Social Services, now The Nugent Society, have already developed some of their former CHEs so that they are now jointly registered, as special schools with the DES and CHEs with the Department of Health (formerly known as the Department of Health and Social Security), although these are not schools specifically for delinquents. This would suggest that the voluntaries would be able to be encouraged to lead the way in these developments.

The title 'community home' has not been popular, has been confusing, and should be changed. It has always been a misnomer that did not really describe the facility.

There is an understandable wariness about the management of residential child care resources in the light of recent notorious events. The Pindown affair in Staffordshire (1991) seems to have been born of desperation by ill-informed senior management who were attempting to contain children with behavioural problems. They clearly lacked the skill or the knowledge needed to cope in an acceptable way. The Beck affair in Leicestershire (1991), which is still the subject of a number of post mortem, demonstrates the need to be forever vigilant to the prospect of unscrupulous people gaining entrance to a service where, in the guise of caring for children, they can exploit them for their own perverse needs.

The rapid closure of a network of specialist residential services has inevitably put great pressure on the remaining resources which were, for the most part, established and staffed to deal with children with less complex needs than those for whom they are now caring. The virtual elimination of a resource in which some people were able to achieve professional advancement within the residential child care service has considerably reduced the pool of experienced and knowledgeable people from which to draw managers for residential child care facilities and so make it more likely that senior managers will, as in the case of 'Pindown', lack the necessary skills to cope correctly with the pressures of the work.

If the CHE system is not to collapse and vanish then some

fresh initiatives have to be developed. A new constructive approach, such as the one outlined above, would be a way of enabling young delinquents to be managed and contained in a setting other than the penal and secure institutions, when it is necessary to remove them from society for a time. This, broadly, was the concept reluctantly acknowledged in the first instance by the Victorians and then adapted by all subsequent generations until the late 1970s. It surely is open to question whether such a tradition should have been so rapidly and easily cast aside.

John Gittins, who did so much to give the Approved Schools a sense of purpose and who had such high expectations of the effects that would flow from the 1969 Children's Act, wrote that he believed the 1969 Act was:

> *...one of the noblest pieces of legislation ever devised, but has been so lamentably implemented as to achieve, in some of its most important provisions, the opposite to what was intended (Gittins, 1985).*

Gittins suggested that, in addition, a number of other factors added to the decline of the CHEs. These were 'social work ideology, union rigidity and local authority ignorance of this field'. Even the title Community Home with Education on the premises, he held, proved to be 'so inept as to be lethal'. One might as well call a monastery 'a workhouse with religion on the premises'. He concluded that:

> *Meanwhile thousands of children are incarcerated in penal establishments which were never intended for them and for which, please God, they were never intended.*

These last words could have been written in the early part of the nineteenth century by Mary Carpenter or Matthew Davenport Hill. The main difference is that, in their time, the options were much clearer whereas today they are clouded by often illusory solutions. Some important lessons have to be learnt from what has been cast aside if a truly comprehensive system of managing child delinquents is to be sustained.

Appendix A: Institutions Which Changed from Approved School to Community Home Status in 1973.

(B - Boys School; G - Girls School; CC - County Council; LBC - London Borough Council; LA - Local Authority; CBC - County Borough Council)

School	Management Body	Community Home Status
Ardale (B)	Was Essex CC became Newham LBC	LA
Avalon (G)	Salvation Army to Bromley LBC	Assisted
Ave Maria (G)	Local Committee to Greenwich LBC	Assisted
Avonside (G)	Local Committee to Somerset CC	Controlled
Axwell Park (B)	Local management to Newcastle upon Tyne CBC	Controlled
Aycliffe (B)	Local management to Durham CC	Controlled
Banstead Hall (B)	LA to Surrey CC	LA
Benton Grange (G)	Local Committee Newcastle upon Tyne CBC	Assisted
Blackbrook Hse (G)	Local Committee Lancashire CC	Assisted
Boreatton Park (B)	Assisted Committee to Salop CC	LA
Bryanston House (G)	Church Army	Assisted
Bryn Esyn (B)	Local Committee to Denbighshire CC	LA
Bryn-y-Don (B)	Cardiff and Glamorgan CC	LA
Carlton (B)	Local Committee to Bedfordshire CC	Controlled
Castle (B)	Local Committee to Teesside LBC	Controlled
Castle Howard (B)	Kingston upon Hull CBC	LA
Chafford (B)	Essex CC	LA
Chaworth (G)	Local Committee to Camden LBC	LA
Crescent, The (G)	Bristol CBC	LA
Cotswold (B)	The Rainer Foundation to Wiltshire CC	LA
Court Lees (B) (became Hayes Bridge)	Local Committee to Surrey CC	LA
Danesbury (B)	Hertfordshire CC	LA
Danesford (B)	National Children's Home - Cheshire CC	Assisted
Desford (B) (became Polebrook House)	Leicestershire CC	LA
Dobroyd Castle (B)	Local Committee to Yorkshire West Riding CC	LA
Druids Heath (B)	Barnardos to Walsall CBC	Assisted
Duncroft (G)	National Association for Mental Health to Hounslow LBC	Assisted
Eagle House (B)	Local Committee to Somerset CC	Controlled
East Moor (B)	Local Committee to Leeds CBC	LA
Edmond Castle (B)	Local Committee to Cumberland CC	Controlled
Egerton House (B)	Local Committee to Northamptonshire CC	Controlled
Essex Homes (B)	Local Committee to Essex CC	Controlled
Farnsworth/St Aidans (B)	Liverpool Catholic Training Schools Association to Liverpool CBC	Assisted
Farringdon House (G)	Local Committee to Devon CC	Controlled
Finnart House (B)	Local Committee to Hammersmith LBC	Controlled
Forde Park (B)	Local Committee to Devon CC	Controlled
Fylde The (B)	Local Committee to Lancashire CC	Controlled
Glamorgan Farm (B)	Glamorgan CC	LA
Greenacres (G)	Local Committee to Wiltshire CC	Controlled
Greenfield House (B)	Liverpool Training Schools to Lancashire CC	Assisted
Greystone Heath (B)	Liverpool CBC	LA
Headlands (B)	National Children's Home to Glamorgan CC	Assisted
Herts Training (B)	Herts Training Ltd to Hertfordshire CC	Controlled
Hyrstslands (G)	Salvation Army to Yorkshire West Riding CC	Assisted
Jordens Bank (G)	Gloucestershire CC	LA

Kerrison (B)	Local Committee to East Suffolk CC	Controlled
Kingswood (B)	Local Committee to Bristol	LA
Kneesworth Hall (B)	Local Committee to Cambridgeshire, Isle of Ely	Controlled
Knotley House (B)	Dr Barnardos to Kent CC	Assisted
Knowle Hill (G)	Local Committee to Warwickshire CC	Controlled
Longfords (G)	Church Moral Aid to Gloucestershire CC	Controlled
Longhirst Hall (B)	Local Committee to Northumberland CC	Controlled
Mayford (B)	Surrey CC	LA
Mile Oak (B)	East Sussex CC	LA
Mobberley (B)	Manchester CBC	LA
Moorland House (B)	Bradford CBC	LA
Moorside (G)	Sheffield CBC	Controlled
National Nautical (B)	National Nautical School to Bristol CBC	Controlled
Netherton (B)	Local Committee to Northumberland CC	Controlled
Newfield House (G)	Local Committee to Coventry CC	LA
Northbrook (B)	Local Committee to Devon CC	Controlled
North Downs (B)	Kent CC	LA
Netherdene Rd (G)	Local Committee to Manchester CBC	Controlled
Northumberland Village Homes (G)	Local Committee to Tynemouth LBC	Controlled
Norton (B)	Local Committee to Warwickshire CC	Controlled
Park House	Became special school	
Pelham House (B)	Local Committee to Cumberland CC	Controlled
Pishiobury (B)	Hertfordshire CC	LA
Poplar Bank House (B)	Local Committee to Lancashire CC	Controlled
Princess Mary VH (G)	Local Committee to Merton LBC	Controlled
Quinta (B)	Barnardos to Shropshire CC	
Red Bank (B)	Red Bank Schools Ltd to Lancashire CC	Controlled
Red House (B)	Local Committee to Norfolk CC	Controlled
Richmond Hill (B)	Local Committee to Yorkshire North Riding CC	LA
Risley Hall (B)	Nottinghamshire CC	LA
Rowley Hall (G)	Local Committee to Staffordshire CC	Controlled
Royal Philanthropic (B)	Royal Philanthropic Society to Wandsworth LBC	Controlled
Ryalls Court (G)	National Children's Home to Devon CC	Assisted
St Benedicts (B)	Brothers of Christian Schools to Brent LBC	LA
St Camillus (B)	Local Committee to Yorkshire West Riding CC	Assisted
St Christophers Hayes (B)	Hillingdon LBC	LA
St Christophers Home (G)	Local Committee to Liverpool LBC	Controlled
St Edwards (B)	Local Committee to Hampshire	Assisted
St Euphrasias (G)	Good Shepherd Sisters to Monmouthshire	Assisted
St Georges (B)	Liverpool Catholic Children's Society to Liverpool	Assisted
St Gilberts (B)	Brothers of Christian Schools to Worcestershire CC	Assisted
St Hildas Apethorp (B)	Northants Catholic Children's Society to Northamptonshire CC	Controlled
St Johns Home Bi'ham (G)	Daughters of Charity	Assisted
St Johns Tiffield (B)	Local Committee to Northamptonshire CC	Controlled
St Johns Wakefield (G)	St Johns Wakefield to Yorkshire West Riding CC	Controlled
St Josephs Ashwicke (G)	Good Shepherd Sisters to Bristol CBC	Assisted
St Josephs (B)	Nentwich Brothers of Christian Schools to Cheshire CC	LA
St Lawrences (G)	Sisters of Sacred Heart	Assisted
St Peters Gainford (B)	Hexham & Newcastle Rescue Society to Teeside CBC	Assisted
St Swithins Nautical (B)	Brothers of Christian Schools to Hampshire.	LA
St Thomas More (B) Birkdale	Liverpool Catholic Training Schools to Lancashire CC	Assisted
St Thomas More (B) W. Grinstead	Southwark Catholic Childrens Society to Southwark LBC	Assisted
St Vincents Dartford (B)	Southwark Catholic Childrens Society to Lewisham LBC	Assisted

St Vincents Formby (B)	Liverpool Catholic Training Schools to Liverpool CBC	Assisted
St Vincents Tankerton (B)	Southwark Catholic Childrens Society to Bexley LBC	Assisted
St Williams (B)	Local Committee to Yorkshire East Riding CC	Assisted
Sedbury Park (B)	Local Committee to Gloucestershire CC	Controlled
Shadwell (B)	Leeds CBC	LA
Shawberry	Birmingham CBC	LA
Shermanbury Grange (G)	West Sussex CC	LA
Skegley Hall (B)	Nottinghamshire CC	LA
Springhead Park (G)	National Association for Mental Health to Yorkshire West Riding CC	Assisted
Stainthwaite Ghyll (B)	Local Committee to Westmorland CC	LA
Stockton Hall (B)	York CBC	LA
Tennal (B)	Local Committee to Birmingham CBC	LA
Thorparch (B)	Leeds CBC	LA
Ty Mawr (B)	Breconshire CC	LA
Walsh Manor (B)	East Sussex CC	LA
Wellesley Nautical (B)	Local Committee to Sunderland CBC	Controlled
Werrington (B)	Staffordshire CC	LA
West Bank	Salford Catholic Rescue Society to Stockport CBC	Assisted
Winton House (B)	Hampshire CC	LA
Woodlands (G)	Salvation Army to East Sussex CC	Assisted

Sources of Data: *Directory of Approved Schools, HMSO 1965*
Community Schools Gazette, November 1973
Directory of Community Homes by Association of Community Homes, 1981.

Appendix B: Region 1, Community Homes with Education, Running Costs, 1980-81

	Boys & Girls	Boys							Girls			
Group / Age	8yrs & over	8yrs & over				12yrs & over	14yrs & over		10yrs & over	12yrs & over	14yrs & over	
Institution	Aycliffe Training	Castle	Longhirst Hall	Pelham House	St Peters	Axwell Park	Edmond Castle	Wellesley	North'land Village Homes	Benton Grange	St, Hildas	Beacon Hill
1. Associated Local Authority	Durham	Cleveland	North'land	Cumbria	Cleveland	Newcastle	Cumbria	Sunderland	N Tyneside	Newcastle	Newcastle	North'land
2. Status	Controlled	Controlled	Controlled	Controlled	Assisted	Controlled	Controlled	Controlled	Controlled	Assisted	Controlled	LA
	£	£	£	£	£	£	£	£	£	£	£	£
EXPENDITURE:-												
3. Employees	425,402	288,643	284,742	231,951	375,259	325,505	209,035	445,598	382,628	270,395	201,915	192,691
4. Premises	98,703	23,999	39,486	35,254	90,749	75,466	45,388	80,791	82,395	55,987	31,292	20,606
5. Supplies and services	53,850	22,854	32,929	39,652	82,514	25,546	36,449	62,795	40,688	58,558	24,623	18,053
6. Transport	7,378	10,043	3,123	4,903	8,487	7,260	7,232	12,232	6,950	6,585	1,051	3,330
7. Establishment expenses	6,489	5,418	4,782	4,300	20,371	9,612	5,658	9,836	10,217	15,386	5,249	3,197
8. Miscellaneous expenses	5,274	2,274	3,965		21	3,203	562		1,919	8,467	3,803	4,860
9. Debt charges	2,490	1,979	2,451	1,095	8,110	9,688	1,016 cr	32,590	14,165	5,593	2,434	135,767
10. Revenue contributions to capital outlay	-	-	-	-	11,172	-	-	-	-	-	-	-
11. Gross expenditure	599,586	355,210	371,478	317,155	596,683	456,280	303,308	643,842	538,962	420,971	270,367	378,504
LESS INCOME:-												
12. Staff board, meals, rents etc	8,128	3,383	5,619	8,645	7,822	7,879	5,034	6,390	4,909	160	3,598	1,915
13. NET EXPENDITURE	591,458	351,827	365,859	308,510	588,861	448,401	298,274	637,452	534,053	420,811	266,769	376,589
14. Days used	20,671	14,521	15,232	19,575	17,764	12,747	10,834	22,010	16,894	13,757	11,613	8,984
15. Weekly cost per place used	200.84	170.07	168.60	110.63	232.68	246.91	193.25	203.29	221.89	214.71	161.24	294.23
16. Weekly charge	156.80	79.18	125.58	97.02	162.23	189.62	106.54	168.35	223.02	212.14	202.60	259.14
17. Percentage occupancy	94	56	64	83	62	58	49	67	84	94	99	103

Appendix C: Region 1, Community Homes with Education, Costs to Local Authorities, 1980-81

	Boys & Girls				Boys						Girls	
	8yrs & over				8yrs & over	12yrs & over	14yrs & over		10yrs & over	12yrs & over	14yrs & over	
	Aycliffe Training	Castle	Longhirst Hall	Pelham House	St Peters	Axwell Park	Edmond Castle	Wellesley	North'land Village Homes	Benton Grange	St Hildas	Beacon Hill
1. Associated Local Authority	Durham	Cleveland	North'land	Cumbria	Cleveland	Newcastle	Cumbria	Sunderland	N Tyneside	Newcastle	Newcastle	North'land
	£	£	£	£	£	£	£	£	£	£	£	£
2. Net Expenditure (line 13 on Statement of Actual Income and Expenditure 1980/81 - Statement A)	591,458	351,827	365,859	308,510	588,861	448,401	298,274	637,452	534,053	420,811	266,769	376,589
3. LESS: Contributions from Local Authorities	464,387	164,252	273,262	274,262	417,119	350,305	164,894	533,814	515,519	457,982	332,941	332,588
4. Deficit/Surplus (Cr)	127,071	187,575	92,597	34,248	171,742	98,096	133,380	103,638	18,534	37,171 cr	66,172 cr	44,001
Apportionment of Deficit Between Local Authorities in No. 1 Area												
5. Cleveland	24,479	36,127	17,838	6,598	33,077	18,897	25,694	19,965	3,570	7,161 cr	12,747 cr	8,476
6. Cumbria	14,717	21,721	10,725	3,967	19,888	11,361	15,448	12,003	2,147	4,305 cr	7,664 cr	5,096
7. Durham	20,036	29,581	14,600	5,400	27,084	15,468	21,031	16,341	2,922	5,861 cr	10,434 cr	6,938
8. Gateshead	6,905	10,185	5,031	1,861	9,326	5,330	7,247	5,631	1,007	2,020 cr	3,596 cr	2,391
9. Newcastle	22,410	33,088	16,330	6,040	30,295	17,300	23,523	18,278	3,269	6,555 cr	11,670 cr	7,760
10. N Tyneside	10,327	13,355	6,594	2,439	12,228	6,986	9,498	7,380	1,320	2,647 cr	4,712 cr	3,133
11. Northumberland	9,049	15,250	7,525	2,783	13,962	7,972	10,840	8,423	1,506	3,021 cr	5,378 cr	3,576
12. S Tyneside	7,856	11,592	5,725	2,117	10,614	6,065	8,246	6,407	1,146	2,298 cr	4,091 cr	2,721
13. Sunderland	11,292	16,676	8,229	3,043	15,268	8,717	11,853	9,210	1,647	3,303 cr	5,880 cr	3,910
14. TOTAL	127,071	187,575	92,597	34,248	171,742	98,096	133,380	103,638	18,534	37,171 cr	66,172 cr	44,001

Appendix D: Community Homes with Education Closed from 1978-1990

Name	Local Authority (with Voluntary Agency where applicable)

Boys

Name	Local Authority
Axwell Park	Newcastle
Blackburn House	Lancs
Carlton	Bedfordshire
Chafford Park	Essex
Crouchfield	Herts
Dobroyd Castle	Humberside
Eagle House	Somerset
Edmond Castle	Cumbria
Egerton House	Northants
Essex Homes	Essex
Farnworth, St Aidans	Liverpool (Catholic Vol)
Finnart House	Hammersmith
Forde Park	Devon
Greenfield House	St Helens
Greystone Heath	Liverpool
Kneesworth House	Cambridgeshire
Kinton	Surrey
Longhirst Hall	Northumberland
Mile Oak	East Sussex
National Nautical	Avon
Northbrook	Devon
Norton	Warwickshire
Pelham House	Cumbria
Pishiobury	Herts
Polebrook House	Leicestershire
Royal Philanthropic	Wandsworth
Quinta	Shropshire (Barnados)
Richmond Hill	North Yorkshire
Risley Hall	Notts
Rowley Hall	Staffs
St Benedicts	Brent
St Camillus	North Yorks (Catholic Vol)
St Christophers	Hillingdon
St Georges	Sefton (Catholic Vol)
St Gilberts	Hereford & Worcs
St Peters	Cleveland (Catholic Vol)
St Thomas More	Southwark (Catholic Vol)
St Thomas More	Sefton (Catholic Vol)
St Vincents	Lewisham (Catholic Vol)
Sedbury Park	Gloucestershire
Shadwell Park	Leeds
Stockton Hall	North Yorks

Tennal	Birmingham
Walsh Manor	East Sussex
West Glam Farm	West Glamorgan

Girls

Ave Maria	Greenwich (Catholic Vol)
Beacon Hill	Northumberland
Benton Grange	Newcastle (Catholic Vol)
Crescent	Avon
Duncroft	Barnardos
Eton Lodge	Liverpool (Catholic Vol)
Farringdon	Devon
Hystlands	Kirklees (Salvation Army)
Moorside	Sheffield
Newfield House	Coventry
Northdene	Manchester
Northumberland Village Homes	North Tyneside
St Christophers	Liverpool
St Edwards	Hampshire
St Josephs	Wiltshire
Silverbrook House	Mid Glam
Southwood	LB Lambeth
Springhead Park	Barnados
Summerlands	Hampshire
Woodlands	West Sussex

Mixed

Apethorpe (St Johns)	Northants
Danesbury	Herts
Greenacres	Wiltshire
Headlands	South Glamorgan (NCH)
Kingswood	Avon
Long Close	Derby
Mill House	Cumbria
Red House	Norfolk
Ryalls Court	Devon (NCH)
St Hildas	Newcastle
St Josephs	Cheshire
Saxon House	Lincs

Appendix E: Community Homes with Education Remaining Open in 1990

Boys	Managing Agency
Ardale	London Borough of Newham
Aycliffe	Durham
Bryn Estyn	Clwyd
Cotswold Community	Wilts/Walsall
Danesbury	NCH/Leics
Eastmoor	Leeds
Flyde School	Lancs
Kerrison	Suffolk
Kingswood	Avon
Kinton	Surrey
Knotley House	London Borough of Bromley
Norton	Warwickshire
Red Bank	Lancs
Riverside	Staffs
St Williams	Middlesbrough Catholic Child Welfare/ Humberside
Thorparch Grange	Leeds
Ty Mawr	Gwent
Wellesley	Sunderland

Girls	Managing Agency
Blackbrook House	Liverpool Catholic Services/St Helens
Briars Hey	Lancs
Chaworth	London Borough of Camden
Frant Court	London Borough of Greenwich
Meadowcroft	Lancs
Popular Bank	Lancs

Appendix F: Information Schedule Regarding Closure of Community Homes with Education (Sent to Selected Sample of Heads and Providers, October 1986)

(1)   Organisation detailing
          Name of CHE
          Location
          Address
          Date of establishment
          Intake area
          Sex and age range
          Number of places

(2)   Specialisations (in training and education)

(3)   Staffing structure
          Number of staff
          Length of time in post

(4)   Building - layout - facilities

(5)   Finance costs at the time of closure
          Saving resulting from closure

(6)   Closure process
          Reasons given for closure
          Length of time from announcement to closure
          Impact on residents
          Impact on staff
          Impact on local community
          Impact on board of management
          Subsequent use of property

Appendix G: Information Schedule on the Closure of Community Homes with Education (Sent to All Local Authorities in Management of CHEs)

(1)   Name of CHE responsible body

(2)   Closure date

(3)   Reasons for closure

(4)   Outcome for staff

(5)   Subsequent use of building

Bibliography

Adams, R., Allard, S., Baldwin, J. and Thomas, T. (1981) *A Measure of Diversion?* National Youth Bureau.

Albermarle (1958) *The Youth Service in England and Wales*. The Albermarle Committee. London: Ministry of Health, HMSO.

Association of Directors of Social Services (1985) *Children Still in Trouble*.

Association of Headmasters, Headmistresses and Matrons of Approved Schools (1969) *Approved Schools, 1969, A Study of Development*.

Association of Managers and the Associations of Headmasters, Headmistresses and Matrons and The National Association of Approved Schools (1966) 'Staffs observations on the White Paper', *The Child The Family and The Young Offender*, September.

Bacon, A., MP (1965) 'Address to Residential Child Care Annual Conference', *Child In Care*, December, p.11.

Bakal, Y. (ed.) (1973) *Closing Correctional Institutions*. Mass, USA: Lexington Book.

Banner, G. (1979) 'Staff Management' in *Changing Patterns of Management of CHEs*. DHSS.

Banner, G. and Kahan, B. (1969) *The Residential Task in Child Care*. The Castle Priory Report. Residential Child Care Association.

Black (1979) *Report of the Children and Young Persons Review Group, Belfast*. The Black Report. HMSO

Bruce, M. (1973) *The Rise of The Welfare State*. London: Weidenfeld & Nicholson.

Burns, J. (1977) 'The expectations of residential care and alternatives', *Community Schools Gazette*, January.

Carlebach, J. (1967) *Caring For Children In Trouble*. Second Edition. London: Routledge & Kegan Paul.

Carlton School Report (1960) *Disturbances at the Carlton School on 29 and 30 August 1959*. HMSO.

Carpenter, M. (1851; 1968) *Reformatory Schools for Children of the Perishing and Dangerous Classes*. London. Facsimile Reprint Gilspin, Woburn Press.

Carpenter, M. (1853) *Juvenile Delinquents, Their Conditions and Treatment*. London.

Cawson, P. (1978) *Community Homes: A Study of Residential Staff*. London: HMSO.

Community Home Schools Gazette (1978) 'A statement by social work agencies on the Children and Young Persons Act 1969, an interim evaluation', May.

Cooper, J. (1976) 'Closing the training schools in Massachusetts', *Social Work Service Journal*, July.

Cooper, J. (1980) 'Retrospect and prospect', *Community Homes Gazette*, December.

Cornish, D.B. and Clarke, R.V.G. (1975) *Residential Treatment and Its Effects on Delinquency*. London: HMSO.

Curtis (1946) *The Care of Children Committee*. The Curtis Report. London: HMSO.

Denne, J. and Peel, R. (1981) 'Does IT work', *Community Care*, 17 March.

Denton, M. (1980) 'Change and chance', *Community Homes Gazette*, December.

Department of Education and Science (1980) *Community Homes with Education*. London: HMSO.

Department of Health (1991) *Children in Care in England and Wales March 1989*. London: HMSO.

Department of Health and Social Security (1970) *Care and Treatment in a Planned Environment*. London: HMSO.

Department of Health and Social Security (1972a) *Guide to Intermediate Treatment*. London: HMSO.

Department of Health and Social Security (1972b) *From Approved School to Community Home, St Gilberts*. London: HMSO.

Department of Health and Social Security (1975a) *Community Home Exercise at Carlton*. London: HMSO.

Department of Health and Social Security (1975b) *Seminar on CHEs*. London: HMSO.

Department of Health and Social Security (1976a) *Developments at Risley Hall Community Home*. London: HMSO.

Department of Health and Social Security (1976b) *Approved School to Community Home, St Vincents*. HMSO.

Department of Health and Social Security (1977) *Management of Community Homes with Education on the Premises*. London: HMSO.

Department of Health and Social Security (1979) *A Community Home Growing Up: Developments at St Christophers Hillingdon. 1973-77*. London: HMSO.

DHSS *See* Department of Health and Social Security

Dunlop, A.B. (1974) *The Approved School Experience*. London: HMSO.

Ebert, F. (1960) 'Doubt and expectancy', *The Approved School Gazette*,

January.

Evans, D.H.G. (1975) 'The President's address', *Community Homes Schools Gazette*, December.

Ford, D. (1975) *Children, Courts and Caring*. London: Constable.

Gill, O. (1974) *Whitegate - An Approved School in Transition*. Liverpool: Liverpool University Press.

Gittins, J. (1952) *Approved School Boys*. London: HMSO.

Gittins, J. (1968a) 'Approved schools and the future', *Approved School Gazette*, May.

Gittins, J. (1968b) 'Children in trouble', *Approved School Gazette*, June.

Gittins, J. (1985) 'Foreword', *The Best of The Gazette*. Social Care Association.

Hazel, N. and Cox, R. (1973) 'Put them back', *Residential Social Work*, 1 July.

Henderson, A.J. (1968) 'Foresight saga', *Approved School Gazette*, June.

Heywood T. (1965) *Children In Care*. London: Routledge and Kegan Paul.

Home Office (1951) *Sixth Report of the Children's Department*. London: HMSO.

Home Office (1955) *Seventh Report of the Children's Department*. London: HMSO.

Home Office (1961) *Eighth Report of the Children's Department*. London: HMSO.

Home Office (1965) *The Child, The Family and The Young Offender*. London: HMSO.

Home Office (1966) *Report of the Work of the Children's Department 1964-66*. London: HMSO.

Home Office (1968) *Children in Trouble*. London: HMSO.

Home Office (1969) *Report of the Work of the Children's Department 1967-69*. London: HMSO.

Home Office (1985) *The Cautioning of Offenders*. Circular 14. London: HMSO.

Home Office Children's Department (1961) *A Handbook for Managers of Approved Schools*. London: HMSO.

Home Office Research Unit (1971) *Absconding From Approved Schools*. London: HMSO.

Hyland, J. (1986) 'More harm than good', *Insight: Social Service Management Journal*, 26 November.

Ingleby (1960) *Report of the Committee on Children and Young Persons*. The Ingleby Report. London: HMSO.

Jenkins, V. (1987) *Community Homes With Education: A Decade of Decline. A Study of One CHE 1976-1986*. Unpublished MEd

Thesis, University of Newcastle upon Tyne.

Johnston, D.D. (1960) *The History of and Development of Approved School Treatment*. Unpublished Thesis, University of Durham/ Newcastle.

Jones, S. (1985) *Polebrook House: A Community Home with Education. The Closure, A Personal Perspective*. Unpublished.

Kilbrandon (1964) *Scottish Home and Health Department Report on Children and Young Persons (Scotland)*. The Kilbrandon Report. London: HMSO.

Knapp, M. and Fengo, A. (1984) *Residential Care In the Voluntary Sector - Demand and Supply. Explanations of Fee and Utilization Variations*. Discussion Paper 378, University of Kent.

Lane, D. (1968) *The Public Image of The Approved School System*. Unpublished Study, University of Newcastle upon Tyne, May.

Levy, A. and Kahan, B. (1991) *The Pindown Experience and the Protection of Children*. The Pindown Report. Staffordshire County Council.

Logan-Salton, M. (1984) *Juvenile Crime: Institutions for Young Offenders*. London: The Monday Club.

Longford (1964) *Crime - A Challenge to Us All*. The Longford Report. Labour Party.

Millham, S., Bullock, R. and Cherrett, P. (1975) *After Grace Teeth*. London: Human Context Books.

Mind (1975) *The Act on Trial*. Report 14. London: The Mental Health Movement.

Morris, A., Gillen, H., Szwed E. and Geach, H. (1980) *Justice For Children*. London: Macmillan.

NACRO *See* National Association for the Care and Resettlement of Offenders

National Association for the Care and Resettlement of Offenders (1984) *Juvenile Crime Consultative Group*. Liverpool Review.

National Association for the Care and Resettlement of Offenders (1985a) *Juvenile Crime*.

National Association for the Care and Resettlement of Offenders (1985b) *Burglary*.

National Association for the Care and Resettlement of Offenders (1985c) *Juvenile Crime Consultative Group*. Sunderland Review.

National Association for the Care and Resettlement of Offenders (1985d) *Juvenile Crime Consultative Group*. Kingston upon Hull.

National Association for the Care and Resettlement of Offenders (1985e) *Juvenile Crime Consultative Group*. Reading.

National Association for the Care and Resettlement of Offenders

(1985f) *Juvenile Crime Consultative Group*. London Borough of Newham.

National Association for the Care and Resettlement of Offenders (1985g) *Juvenile Crime Consultative Group*. Teesside.

National Association for the Care and Resettlement of Offenders (1986) *Juvenile Crime: Coordination and the Community*.

National Association for the Care and Resettlement of Offenders (1987) *Time for Change*. London.

Newson (1963) *Half Our Future*. The Newson Report. London: HMSO.

North West Region Social Services Agencies (1981a) *Community Provision for Young Offenders*. Department of Health and Social Security.

North West Region Social Services Agencies (1981b) *Quality of Care Project*. Department of Health and Social Security.

Packman, J. (1981) *The Child's Generation*. Oxford: Blackwell & Morrison.

Parliamentary All Party Penal Affairs Group (1981) *Young Offenders: A Strategy for the Future*. London: HMSO.

Pinchbeck, I. and Hewitt, M. (1973) *Children in English Society*. Volume 2. London: Routledge & Kegan Paul.

Plowden (1966) *Children and Their Primary Schools*. The Plowden Report. London: HMSO.

Read, D. (1979) *England 1868-1914*. London: Longman.

Reader, W.J. (1974) *Victorian England*. London: Book Club Associates, by arrangement with B.T. Batsford Ltd.

Redcliffe-Maud (1969) *Royal Commission on Local Government*. London: HMSO.

Residential Child Care Association (1970) *The Child In Care*, February.

Reynold (1946) *Approved Schools and Remand Homes, Remuneration and Conditions of Service*. The Reynolds Report. London: HMSO.

Rose, G. (1967) *Schools for Young Offenders*. London: Tavistock Publications.

Rowe, J., Hundleby, M. and Garnett, L. (1989) *Child Care Now*. British Agencies for Adoption & Fostering.

Rowe, J. and Lambert, L. (1973) *Children Who Wait*. Association of British Adoption Agencies.

Seebohm (1968) *Report of the Committee on Local Authority and Allied Personal Social Services*. The Seebohm Report. London: HMSO.

Select Committee for Estimates (1948-49 *Eighteenth Report from the Select Committee for Estimates, Sessions 1948-49. Approved Schools*. London: HMSO.

Short, R. (1975) *Eleventh Report of the Expenditure Committee Session: The Children and Young Persons Act 1969*. Volume 1. The Short Report. London: HMSO.

Stacey, N. (1977) 'Foster care: practicalities and expectations', *Community Home Schools Gazette*, January.

Stevens, M. and Crook, I. (1986) 'What the devil is intermediate treatment?', *Social Work Today*, 8 September.

Thomas, J. (1982) *A Survey of Special Fostering Placements In London*. London Boroughs Regional Planning Committee.

Thorpe D. et al. (1976) *A Study of The Implementation of the 1969 Children's and Young Persons Act*. University of Lancaster.

Thorpe, D., Smith, D., Green, C.T. and Paley, H. (1980) *Out of Care: The Community Support of Juvenile Offender*. Allen & Unwin.

Tutt, N. (1974) *Care or Custody?* London: Dorton, Longman & Todd.

Tutt, N. (1982) 'Justice or welfare?', *Social Work Today,* 19 October.

Tutt, N. and Giller, H. (1985) 'Doing justice to great expectation', *Social Work Today*, 17 January.

Utting, W. (1978) 'Address to Association of Community Homes with Education', *Community Schools Gazette,* December.

Utting (1991) *Children in the Public Care*. The Utting Report. London: HMSO.

Wagner (1988a) *Residential Care: A Positive Choice. The Wagner Report*. London: National Institute for Social Work, HMSO.

Wagner (1988b) *Residential Care: The Research Reviewed. The Wagner Report*. Volume 2. London: National Institute for Social Work, HMSO.

Warnock (1978) *Report of the Committee of Enquiry into Education of Handicapped Children and Young People: Special Educational Needs*. The Warnock Report. London: HMSO.

White, T. (1965) *Child Care News*, October.

Williams (1967) *Caring for People*. The Williams Report. National Council for Social Services. London: George Allen & Unwin.

Wilson, J.L. (1965) 'Relevant aspects of the Kilbrandon Report, *Approved School Gazette,* January.

Younghusband (1959) *Report of the Working Party on Social Workers in Local Authority Health and Welfare Services. The Younghusband Working Party*. London: Ministry of Health, Department of Health for Scotland, HMSO.

Legislation Referred to in the Text

Factory Act, 1819
Factory Act, 1833
Poor Law Amendment Act, 1834
Mines Act, 1842
Reformatory Schools (Youthful Offenders) Act, 1854
Industrial Schools Act, 1857
Education Act, 1870
Education Act, 1880
Probation of First Offenders Act, 1887
Reformatory Schools Act, 1899
Youthful Offenders Act, (1901)
Probation of Offenders Act, 1907
Children Act, 1908
Children and Young Persons Act, 1933
Children and Young Persons Act, 1948
Criminal Justice Act, 1961
Children and Young Persons Act, 1963
Social Work (Scotland) Act, 1968
Children and Young Persons Act, 1969
Local Authority Health and Social Services Act, 1970
Local Government Act, 1972
Criminal Justice Act, 1982
Health and Social Services and Social Security Adjudications Act, 1983
Children Act, 1989
Criminal Justice Act, 1991

Index